Street Angel

Life Writing Series

In the **Life Writing Series**, Wilfrid Laurier University Press publishes life writing and new life-writing criticism and theory in order to promote autobiographical accounts, diaries, letters, and testimonials written and/or told by women and men whose political, literary, or philosophical purposes are central to their lives. The Series features accounts written in English, or translated into English from French or the languages of the First Nations, or any of the languages of immigration to Canada.

From its inception, **Life Writing** has aimed to foreground the stories of those who may never have imagined themselves as writers or as people with lives worthy of being (re)told. Its readership has expanded to include scholars, youth, and avid general readers both in Canada and abroad. The Series hopes to continue its work as a leading publisher of life writing of all kinds, as an imprint that aims for both broad representation and scholarly excellence, and as a tool for both historical and autobiographical research.

As its mandate stipulates, the Series privileges those individuals and communities whose stories may not, under normal circumstances, find a welcoming home with a publisher. **Life Writing** also publishes original theoretical investigations about life writing, as long as they are not limited to one author or text.

Series Editor
Marlene Kadar
Humanities Division, York University

Manuscripts to be sent to
Lisa Quinn, Acquisitions Editor
Wilfrid Laurier University Press
75 University Avenue West
Waterloo, Ontario N2L 3C5
Canada

Street Angel

Magie Dominic

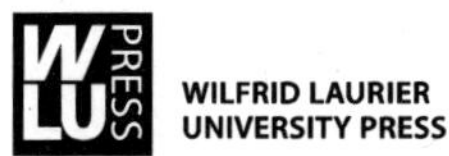

Wilfrid Laurier University Press acknowledges the support of the Canada Council for the Arts for our publishing program. We acknowledge the financial support of the Government of Canada through the Canada Book Fund for our publishing activities.

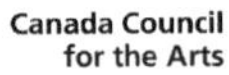

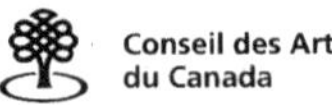

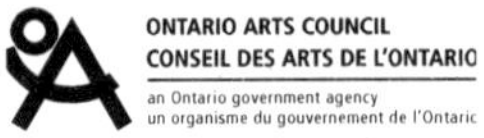

Library and Archives Canada Cataloguing in Publication

Dominic, Magie, 1944–, author
Street angel / Magie Dominic.

(Life writing series)
Issued in print and electronic formats.
ISBN 978-1-77112-026-5 (pbk.).—ISBN 978-1-77112-028-9 (epub).—
ISBN 978-1-77112-027-2 (pdf)

1. Dominic, Magie, 1944–. 2. Dominic, Magie, 1944– —Family. 3. Adult child sexual abuse victims—Canada—Biography. 4. Artists—Canada—Biography. 5. Authors, Canadian (English)—20th century—Biography. 6. Newfoundland and Labrador—Biography. I. Title. II. Series: Life writing series

HV6626.23.C3D645 2014 362.76092 C2014-902722-2
C2014-902723-0

Cover design by Sandra Friesen. Cover image by Magie Dominic: *Discipula, a Female Student* (collage with waxflower petals, cardboard, gouache, rainwater, and a photograph taken by George Dominic in 1949). Text design by Carol Magee.

RECYCLED
Paper made from recycled material
FSC www.fsc.org FSC® C103567

This book is printed on FSC recycled paper and is certified Ecologo. It is made from 100% post-consumer fibre, processed chlorine free, and manufactured using biogas energy.

Printed in Canada

To my daughter Heather Rose
and to the island called Newfoundland

Granted, the ship comes into harbour with shrouds and tackle damaged; the pilot is blameworthy ... but to know how *blameworthy, tell us first whether his voyage has been round the Globe, or only to Ramsgate and the Isle of Dogs.*

Thomas Carlyle, *Carlyle's Essay on Burns*

Suddenly, from behind the rim of the moon, in long, slow-motion moments of immense majesty, there emerges a sparkling blue and white jewel, a light, delicate sky-blue sphere laced with slowly swirling veils of white, rising gradually like a small pearl in a thick sea of black mystery. It takes more than a moment to fully realize this is Earth … home.

Edgar Mitchell, *Apollo 14* astronaut

Contents

Part One

Chapter One

SATURDAY *Day One*

It's 1956. "Tennessee Waltz" on the radio in the kitchen. Ingrid Bergman and Marilyn Monroe. The Russians are sending dogs into space and the dogs have spacesuits and helmets. Ed Sullivan and the show of shows. *The Honeymooners* on Saturday night. Pat Boone and Nat King Cole. Food rationing has ended in England. *Lady and the Tramp* and *Peter Pan.* Elvis Presley appears on TV but we're not allowed to look at his legs. Polio shots in the school auditorium.

It's the summer between grade six and grade seven. I'm eleven years old. A June Saturday afternoon and I'm in my father's blue Chevrolet, on a Newfoundland section of the Trans-Canada Highway, on my way to the home of my father's brother and his wife and their two boys.

My father has heavy snow chains attached to the car's back bumper and the car drags them like the silver tail of a dragon—a dragon travelling at a moderate speed through occasional clouds of dust. Dragging chains from the back of a car prevents anyone in the car from having a sudden attack of car sickness. That's the theory. The technique has never worked for me, but my father attaches the chains every time we go on a trip just in case this is the day that the technique may actually work. My father is always prepared. *A look in front is better than two behind.* My father also has a fully equipped glove compartment. Along with Band-Aids, flashlights, work gloves, and maps, there's a bottle opener for sodas along the way. The glove compartment also has a supply of brochures—my father is a travelling paint salesman—and cards with all the amazing names for a single colour. Strips of cardboard with shades of white—*Bone White, Glossy White, Matte White, Natural Ivory, Medium Ivory, Pure White, Pearl White, Off-White, White.* My father is prepared for a sale right in the middle of the Trans-Canada Highway as it cuts through forest.

My mother is in the front seat. When she was young she was breathtakingly beautiful. I've seen her in black-and-white photographs. Loved to go skating with friends—a graceful figure sailing on ice. She imagined herself a movie star. She smiled often when she was young. Her face is round like a moon and her skin is soft from sweet Jergens lotion. Thick, dark-brown hair. Average height, but she has an air of tallness. Fair Scottish skin. Greenish eyes like a cat. She wears lipstick the colour of pomegranate—*Fire Engine Red.* If the Chinese Communists ever come to our door to take us away, my mother will greet them in *Fire Engine Red.* She looks into mirrors as if she's expecting something to happen—a stranger's face to appear in the glass. Another person—someone she wants to scare or control. Then she does a last-minute flick of her hair, freshens her lipstick, and goes off into town, a whiff of Tweed perfume trailing behind. A part of her lingers. A part of her always remains.

I'm in the back with a small bag. My suitcase is in the trunk next to the spare tire, crowbar, jumper cables, boxes of cookies, and samples of candy. My father is also a travelling confectionery salesman.

I want to be somewhere else for a while—even just for a few days. Away from the madness of home and the nuns. But I'm not sure what I'm doing or why I'm doing it. I'll be staying with my uncle and aunt for nine days, to take care of the two boys—one aged three, the other aged two. They're both plump and lively, and I'm told that they're both good as gold. Got the faces and eyes of angels.

What am I afraid of? I ask myself. It's the unknown. I'll be in charge of two children's lives and I've never been in charge of anything in the entire eleven years of my life. Maybe it's anxiety more than actual fear.

Fear—real, honest-to-God debilitating fear—is an affliction. My mother has the affliction. She lives in absolute fear. Of getting sick, of having an accident, of sounds in the night. She has a debilitating fear of the night. Night is the pinnacle of her affliction. She envisions long, creeping shadows of monsters. She fears a bogeyman under her bed except there is no bogeyman under her bed. She's obsessed with a fear of cancer. My birthday is in July—I'm a Cancer. But my mother maintains that she's the Cancer even though she's a Leo. Fear plays a major part in everything she does. She fears the colour green. That fear has its roots in the Newfoundland fairies. Unlike fairies with magic wands, Newfoundland fairies can cause bodily harm. According to legend, they appeared after the great battle between Lucifer and the archangel Michael.

There were angels in Newfoundland who remained neutral during the battle. When the fighting was over, they were forbidden from heaven because they hadn't supported Michael, but they couldn't be banished to hell because they hadn't supported Lucifer. So they were forced to remain in Newfoundland and can work both evil and good.

They're called The Little People and they live at the edges of towns, in the woods. The only way to protect against their evil is to carry bread—

fairy buns—when going into the woods, and to avoid the colour green. Many believe the bank crash of 1894 was caused because Newfoundland issued a green postage stamp that year.

My mother never wears green and neither do I, nor does my father. There are no green curtains, linens, or dishes. Nothing green enters the house except plants.

My mother fears going hungry. She fears not being smart enough or liked enough or pretty. When she has enough money, she makes a concoction with eggs and lets it harden on her face like a mask. If I come home after school and she's still wearing the mask, I can't ask a question because if she speaks, the mask will crack and the eggs will be wasted. She fears not being strong enough. My mother has so many fears that they've all collided and it's made her crazy.

When my parents were dating, both of their families—the Presbyterian Scots and the Lebanese Catholics—disapproved of their relationship, but primarily the Scots, and to such an extent that my mother had to leave home and move to a rooming house until she and my father were married. All because my father was Lebanese. In pictures he looks like a handsome movie star, but my mother was banished by her own family for wanting to marry him. Romeo and Juliet. My father and my mother. The Lebanese side of the family softened, but the Scots never did. Parts of the Scottish side of the family never entered our house, never walked through the gate. Every time they're invited, they're sick with the flu. If the Lebanese would keep to themselves that would be best for all concerned—that was the feeling among some in my mother's family.

My parents were married in 1943. Non-Catholic partners in marriage have to swear that they'll raise their children in the Catholic faith and not in whatever their own religion might happen to be. That's the rule and everyone, including my mother, abides by it.

In 1943, Newfoundland was recovering from the poverty of the Great Depression, and its economic collapse was tragic. The main export was fish, and the prices for fish plunged. Malnutrition was widespread. People relied on the help of family and friends, but in most cases, one family was as destitute as another. It drove some people insane. I'm told there was no meat in the stores on the day I was born. I'm also told I was born close to midnight—almost the next day.

The year of my birth was 1944. Germany had surrendered Paris, the Soviets had declared war on Bulgaria, the Newfoundland Field Regiment of the Royal Artillery landed in Normandy, Mount Vesuvius had erupted in Italy, and the top song was Bing Crosby's "Swinging on a Star." The world was filled with madness, sadness, and fear. World war, a second time. American bases in Newfoundland and U-boat threats offshore. Ads with soldiers selling toothpaste and Coke. Hitler.

The SS *Caribou,* the Newfoundland ferry boat, torpedoed by German submarines off the Newfoundland coast—137 passengers perished. Mussolini. Detention camps. Concentration camps. Hiroshima. Nagasaki. More than 50 million people are killed worldwide—half of them civilians. Machine guns. Fighter bombers. Light bombers. Heavy bombers. Gasoline restrictions. Abbott and Costello. "White Christmas." Rationed food.

And somewhere in here I was at home and helping with the housework. I was polishing a wooden coffee table—had my own dusting rag and polishing wax. I'm four years old and polish the table until it's glowing—until I can see my own round face in the wood. Then I climb up and stand on top of the oily surface and start to polish the window, slide off the table, onto the floor, and knock myself completely unconscious. I was told I was out for a very long time. I don't know if it was seconds or months. No one defined it.

From the very beginning of time to now, in the back seat of my father's car, it took 600 million years for Newfoundland to rise from the ocean floor. How did I get from the beginning of time to my father's Chevrolet with the chains on the bumper? Count it!

First, the dinosaurs walked on the land. Then the cavemen and someone invented a wheel. Paper was invented. The Roman Empire. Jesus rose from the dead. The Crusades. Black Death. Explorers discovered North America, but the Beothuk were already living here anyway. Explorers filled their boats with millions of fish, stole everything from the Beothuk—including their lives—and settled down and built houses. Gold was discovered in California. Pony Express, telegraphs, and railroads. Small towns and hamlets developed. Each religion built its own church and as the population grew, so did the churches. Each church had its own graveyard so no one got mixed up in heaven. The settlers built shipyards around the coast, including one in my uncle's hamlet.

My father's father, Pop, built two stores. One is in the hamlet and it's managed by my father's brother and we're on our way there in the car. The other store was in our town and managed by my father. There were two different brothers and two different stores in two different towns.

My uncle's hamlet isn't big enough yet to be called anything close to a town. It has at the most five or six hundred people and is nestled in a small sheltered area overlooking a bay. High mountains surround everything. It's an egg in its very own nest, protected by hills and mountains.

You can stand on any hilltop and get a good view—water, sky, and an invisible line upon which approaching ships rest. The wind off the bay feels clean and strong, like a breath of safety.

There's one main street, and everything runs off the street or through it, or is on it already. It's like a self-contained shell with a garage, a drug store, a post office, a grocery store, and a few businesses. There's a small movie theatre that shows films on Saturday afternoons. At one o'clock, cartoons for young children and toddlers—*Casper the Friendly Ghost* or *Popeye*. Then a three o'clock movie for older children and teens—Walt Disney or a film with Bing Crosby or Doris Day. The whirr of a movie projector.

There are two restaurants and a bank. And my uncle's general store.

Everything in the hamlet has room to spread out. Everything is in the act of expanding. Even clouds have more room in the sky. Someone is always adding on to a building—a new roof, a porch, a new set of stairs. There's always some sort of construction. Something being repainted. Large piles of crushed stone for concrete. Roadbeds, culverts, and bridges. There's been construction ever since the hamlet came into being. There are three small churches, all different denominations, and they're all painted white.

Our town has all the businesses of any bustling town. Drug store, post office, and telegraph office. A telephone company. A movie theatre. Charlie Chaplin and Mary Pickford. One summer, a movie about the Blessed Virgin's appearance to Saint Bernadette came to the Majestic Theatre in town. Jennifer Jones saying the rosary. We watched *The Song of Bernadette* and western serials. Gene Autry hanging from a branch overlooking a gulch with absolutely no hope of survival and just as the cliff starts to crumble under his boot, the reel comes to a grinding halt, a sign on the screen says *To Be Continued*, and the screen spins into a news reel about the world events of the week. It was Gene Autry for God's sake. He was infallible. But we couldn't wait until the following Saturday to see how he escaped. Then a fast run to the snack bar—a seven-cent bar or the twelve-cent deluxe, a paper cup of root beer, and hoping the line moved fast so we could get back to our seats before the main feature began.

Our town has several stores and a Chinese restaurant, which burned to the ground one night, taking dozens of businesses and homes along with it. The sky filled with flames like a scene in a Hollywood nightmare—panicked families rushing in silence, men carrying furniture, children with wagons filled with belongings, women carrying babies. And there's a firehouse, which was needed when the Chinese restaurant erupted.

Several businesses are owned by Lebanese families. Clothing, jewellery, and variety shops. Variety shops have seeds in the spring, new brooms when you need them (especially in January—*sweep out the old, sweep in the new*), fishing tackle, stationery, and long bolts of fabric. Dishes and oil for kerosene lamps. Dolls with porcelain heads and sad, glassy eyes—the dolls will cry if you rock them. There's a small shop where people buy Lebanese produce: *kousa*, pine nuts, grape leaves, and Turkish delight. My father buys *kousa* and pine nuts and at Christmas, Turkish delight wrapped in exotic paper with Lebanese lettering. Chip stands. Candy shops. Lebanese-owned clothing and shoe stores.

There are schools for Catholics and schools for the others. You're either Catholic or non-Catholic. If you aren't Catholic, there's no indication of what you might happen to be—you're just non-Catholic. My Lebanese father went to Catholic school. My mother, being Presbyterian, went to the school for the others. I'm being raised Catholic in what the Catholic Church refers to as a *mixed home*—which, in the eyes of the nuns, is one step away from living in sin.

1949. I'm five years old. Frank Sinatra and *The Return of Rin Tin Tin*. The top song is "Buttons and Bows" and Newfoundland joins Canada. Newfoundland's economic crash in the Great Depression, coupled with a profound distrust of politicians, led to the abandonment of self-government. Newfoundland remains the only nation in the entire world to ever voluntarily relinquish its independence. For the well-being of its people, Newfoundland joined Canada in 1949 and we prayed for the new government—for the concern that we were no longer our own country, could no longer have our own Newfoundland money or our own Newfoundland postage stamps—and we prayed for any non-Catholics who were in the dominion. Schools had air-raid shelters and I entered kindergarten. A black tunic with a thin matching belt and a short-sleeved white cotton blouse. Black shoes with straps and short, white cotton socks. Tight ringlets and an enormous white ribbon bow. The bow was almost as big as my head. It exceeded my head, almost like a propeller. Everything in white or black. Heaven or hell.

During the very first week, we had two full pages of homework. A small soft-covered reader with coloured pictures. Page one had a picture of a boy and the word *David* beneath the picture. Page two had a picture of a girl and the word *Ann* beneath the picture. Our homework was to study and learn to read both pages. Completely. I couldn't grasp it—was incapable of understanding the process. I don't know why I was so perplexed over those two pages of literature, but I was. On that evening, the concept of reading the two words *David* and *Ann* was beyond my literary comprehension.

We sat at the table, my mother and I, as she became more and more frustrated with me.

For God's sake, you wouldn't call a boy Ann. Look at the picture! Look at the damn picture. And she flicked her cigarette ash.

Kindergarten at Our Lady of Perpetual Help School was a world of obedience, silence, and penance. Even at five years of age. We were smacked on the hand simply because we could be smacked on the hand. For dropping a pencil. Being late for the bell. For being left-handed—best to beat it out of the child at a very young age. I'm not left-handed but I'm slightly pigeon-toed. God help me. There was a cloakroom with a wooden peg for my coat and I was in class with enormous white ribbon propellers attached to my head.

The nuns, who for the most part and with few exceptions believed they had more power than Jesus, kept me inside the building at recess on a weekly basis when I first started school, instructing me to walk the dim hallway, back and forth, following the straight line of a floorboard with a book on my head.

So I walked back and forth between two towering statues, the Blessed Virgin with her powder-blue sash at one end of the hall and the flaming heart of Jesus at the other, slightly pigeon-toed, with a book on my head.

Look up! Not at the floor! Look up!

It was supposed to make me walk tall and erect and it was supposed to cure my feet. It was supposed to make me feel confident.

I walk with my head lowered most of the time—am quiet most of the time—and I've had a look of operatic tragedy on my face since I was born. I'm prone to an occasional blank stare, I'm slightly pigeon-toed, and I don't really know how to have a conversation with people. I never did.

It's the middle of kindergarten. My grandmother comes to visit us one afternoon. My father's mother. The Lebanese grandmother. My mother tells me to talk with her while she busies herself in the kitchen. *Go talk with your grandmother, Margaret.*

I walk over to my grandmother, who's sitting sombrely in a dining-room chair. My grandmother is extremely fat. There's no way around the fact. She has beautiful soft ivory skin and shiny soft black hair, and she's exceedingly fat and when she sits in a chair she completely conceals the entire piece of furniture, which is exactly what she's doing right now.

I stand in front of my very large grandmother and I speak. *You're wearing the same dress you were wearing the last time you were here.*

My mother flies out of the kitchen.

I'm six years old and in grade one. Our teacher is tall, graceful, beautiful Sister Mary Bernadette. We know absolutely nothing about the nuns in any class, any grade. Maybe the colour of their hair if a few wisps escape the veil, or whether they're fat or short. They all wear the same black billowing habits, all live in the convent next door, all have floor-length straps and rosaries, and they all wear a gold wedding band because they're all married to Jesus.

It's an ordinary day—not my birthday or a feast day. Sister Bernadette walks to my desk and quietly hands me a scapular with a soft, gold, cardboard cover. A small silver medal of the Immaculate Conception is attached with thread to one side, and a plastic, oval-shaped image of the Sacred Heart is attached to the other. The heart is on fire and circled with thorns. The scapular edges are embroidered with minuscule pink and gold stitches—the kind of stitch that can make a person go blind. The two sides are hinged together with the same pink and gold stitch.

Did you make that, Sister? someone asks.

Oh, no! I would never give Margaret something I made myself.

Meaning what? I wonder. *That something she created herself is unworthy of being a gift? Or that I'm not worthy of something she made?*

She doesn't say why I'm the only one to receive a scapular. She doesn't explain anything. She simply puts the scapular on my desk, smiles, and walks away. Maybe it's supposed to make me feel strong. Or cure my ongoing feet problem. Or maybe she was fortifying a child who she knew was in need of fortification.

Anxiety and stress have permanently set into my body, even at six. This gentle nun may have seen everything. This would explain her kindness with every child in her crowded classroom. If we were allowed to remain in her class for the rest of our lives, I doubt any child would relinquish the opportunity. But we'll be forced to move elsewhere.

We're all here to learn and we never know who the teachers will be or what time they'll appear. But if we're vigilant, someone will walk into our lives. This person will be light in the dark. Hope where there was none. We have to pray for this person's appearance. Hope for a miracle. Watch for a saint.

Bernadette probably wasn't a saint, but when you're six years old and there's a moment in life when there's calm and compassion and kindness—especially kindness—and a beautiful embroidered scapular, that's about as close to a saintly environment as any small child can possibly hope for. Small children need warmth and space and time, like a seed. A child is the root of an adult. She knew this. Anyone can be a saint in heaven—you just need two wings and a cloud. Real saints are born here on earth.

There are flowers on the chalkboards in her room in all kinds of weather. Every season. Every holiday. A moon in a starry sky and summer roses. Snowflakes falling on dark earth. Pine cones and poinsettias. In springtime, daffodils and crocuses. Thin pastel lines of green leaves and vines—chalk so light it barely touches the board's surface. In autumn, pumpkins and yellow leaves cover shivering things. A perpetual, glorious landscape revealing itself through a box of coloured chalk.

Grade two. I'm seven years old and there are so many children that we can't all fit in one room, so our class is set up in a large unused portion of the school building—the furnace room, with the actual functioning furnace. A furnace room is meant as a room to minimize the visual impact of a building's heating equipment, but there we are, seventy-two little girls in crisp black-and-white uniforms at Our Lady of Perpetual Help School for one full year with the furnace. Seventy-two little girls and seventy-two wooden desks and one fire-and-brimstone nun keeping order.

If we were silent in kindergarten and grade one, in the furnace room we're immobile. We're told not to move, and we don't. We're told not to speak, and we don't. Hours and hours of silence. The blackboard is on collapsible legs, folded at the end of the day and leaned against the wall—and if we aren't careful, the same thing could happen to us.

If there ever, God forbid, were an accident, a fire in the furnace room, the result would be simply beyond catastrophic. We would all lose our lives when smoke and fire cut off our means of escape through doorways and corridors. We would be killed as we tried to run through the flames. Seventy-two little girls would perish. Along with one heartless nun. Although, as all things go with the nuns, she'd likely escape.

We pray on our knees on the grey concrete floor four times a day, and more during the holy days. Not a single thing changes in the furnace room—not the strappings, the silence, or the obedience. We're just confined with the furnace. And we continue to pray for the souls of all the non-Catholics, including my mother, the Russians, the Communists, the savages, and all the babies in limbo, even though babies in limbo are a hopeless cause. There's more hope for the savages.

We receive First Holy Communion. After weeks of training and memorizing answers about the Host and commandments and blood and water and Latin, and wearing an exquisite white dress and white veil and white shoes and white socks and white gloves and clutching a white rosary and white missal and looking as close to an angel shot straight from heaven as humanly possible, and having landed on a rock called Newfoundland, we are allowed to receive the white Host. For one full day in our lives, we are as pure as God's driven snow. Our souls are spotless and we are without fault. We've received forgiveness for every transgression, every sin we've ever committed. We have received absolution and all is good with the world. That lasts for twenty-four hours—then everything is back to normal.

Right in the middle of grade two, Princess Elizabeth's father dies and the nuns make us kneel on the floor and pray for a very long time. Whenever I think of Queen Elizabeth's father, my knees hurt. Princess Elizabeth becomes the queen and on 18 April, UFOs are seen all over the world. An enormous gold-yellow one is spotted directly over our house. It's in all the papers.

Grade two is the only year in my life that I ever come first, head of the class. I spend a year confined to a room with a functioning furnace, with my bent head and slightly pigeon-toed feet, with my mother's affliction and swearing and fear of the dark, cram my brain with answers, and come first. The furnace room may have had windows but I don't remember seeing them.

Inside our house, my mother's angry most of the time. Bangs cupboard doors and swears. My mother never stops swearing, and not *gosh, darn* words—long phrases of mortal sin words. I don't know if it's because she's Presbyterian or if it's due to the affliction. She fears the demons that stand on the roof and stare through the windows at night. She has an incapacitating fear of the dark. Outdoors, in daylight, in the garden, she's calm and serene. My father, a Catholic, never swears. So I pray for my mother's Presbyterianism and that she'll stop swearing and that the nuns will stop punishing me for the sin of having a non-Catholic mother. For coming from a mixed home. For living in sin.

I'm still seven years old. We're living on Princess Avenue. A different house from the one where I knocked myself unconscious by polishing a table. The yard in back is sloped. There's an enormously high veranda, at least eight feet off the ground, with gravel stones beneath it where there's no sun, and there's a lawn, which tends to be dry. There's a man on one side of the house who saws lumber—hours of sawdust floating through air. Back and forth hum of a saw.

The lawn has plenty of dandelions, which we're eating on a regular basis. Dandelion has a strong bitter taste until I drown it in mustard.

The house is surrounded by a whitewashed picket fence and there's a standard front gate with a sturdy frame. My mother's flowers are in front, against the house, directly below the windows. A row of tall delphiniums in the back of the bed, held up by wooden stakes. Certain flowers can be fatal—the delphinium is one of them. A person has to be careful. It's a bloom that a very small child can easily pick and swallow. Death by blue delphinium. Tall yellow and pink gladioluses with their multiple blooms on one stem. Rows of purple and yellow pansies with their little faces that always seem shocked. Snapdragons and forget-me-nots. The grass in front is soft and thick. There are neighbours close to the fence on one side, and the other side is a road—we're on a corner. A dry lawn and high veranda in back. A soft lawn and flowers in front.

It's Sunday morning and my father and I are at church. The one for the Catholics.

My mother meets us as we get out of the car after Mass and greets us with *Something terrible happened!*

My father says *Pop died!* Pop is his father, once a shop owner in town but an invalid now and deathly ill.

No, worse. Sandy hung himself.

Sandy is my Pekingese dog—a gift from my father's brother and a dog I don't think either my mother or father really wanted. One of them didn't want him. Sandy lives much of his outdoor life tied to a rope on the high veranda.

I've just returned from praying in an incense-filled chapel for over an hour, clutching a rosary and a small starter missal, with hymns and vases of tall altar flowers and the smell of freshly snuffed candles.

While my father and I were praying to Jesus and Mary, Sandy jumped from the veranda after a bone he saw on the ground and hung himself. He jumped from the high porch after a bone, short rope and all. Sandy apparently jumped to his death. This is my mother's theory. Who knows what happened. Who knows what was in that little dog's mind. He may have simply been done with this world. Had seen enough.

My father opens the gate in the white picket fence and we step from the unpaved road, through the gate and into the yard and around to the back and Sandy's dead body dangling at the end of the rope.

My father's brother who gave me the dog is the man who's driving the other car.

I'll be their help in managing the two boys for the first days of vacation, then back home for the rest of the summer. My uncle's house is filled with more furniture than it can possibly manage. The furniture collection is only stopped by the walls.

Before our present house, three houses ago, we visited this hamlet often. At Christmas or Easter or during the summer. Christmas and Easter are big Catholic holidays and the Catholic Lebanese side of the family gathered together and there was an incredible display of food—everything cooked by my father's mother. Lebanese food, Presbyterian food, *kibbeh*, cabbage rolls, *kousa*—dishes for all religions.

We meet at the halfway point on the highway. I remove my suitcase from the trunk. The adults get out of their cars and talk for a few minutes and I step out of one car and into the other and both cars turn around, our car still dragging its chains, and both cars return to their homes and I disappear for nine days. I feel as if I've aged from one car door to the other. This is my first time away from home on my own and my first time being in charge of two people's lives—an uneasy feeling since I have no charge over anyone's life, including my own. But the boys have little clue that I'll be in charge of them during the day, and neither one seems to care in the slightest. This trip was planned by my parents and my aunt and uncle, and after they had all the plans worked out, I was either asked or told.

My uncle is taller than my father, although my father is especially short, so my uncle's height is probably just above average. He has a square jaw and a high, wide forehead. His eyebrows are black and thick. He has thick black wavy hair, a clear complexion, large brown smiling eyes, and a mischievous smile. He looks like a young Charlie Chaplin, without the hat and moustache. He wears wide suspenders and rolls the sleeves of his shirt up to his elbows. He smokes cigars in the evening. All the men on the Lebanese side of the family smoke cigars. There are clouds of white smoke after every meal except breakfast.

My aunt is tall and thin with a pale complexion and light brown hair combed high off her face and pulled back in a soft bun. She has gold-rimmed glasses, a thin gold chain with a crucifix around her neck, and crisply ironed cotton skirts and blouses. My aunt could be a teacher judging by her clothes and the cross at her neck, but she isn't, thank God. I can't figure out what she'll be doing while I'm watching the two boys—maybe working down in the store or occupied somewhere. She'll be home for part of the morning, then gone for part of the afternoon, and I'm in charge of the two boys for those hours. If I need anything, I'm to go to my uncle's store, which, if I walk quickly, is just five minutes away.

I have no hesitation in saying you'll be wonderful with the boys.

I thank her for her trust.

Don't be too alarmed if they cry. Crying is not far away from laughter.

My aunt is exceptionally religious. The kitchen is a combination of linoleum and Jesus: a small wooden crucifix hangs over the sink, *The Last Supper* hangs above the table, and a painting of the Sacred Heart is near the door. So far, I haven't heard her yell at anyone and haven't heard her swear once. If she has, it's been in private.

It's Saturday evening. Supper is over, the boys are in bed, and I'm sitting at the kitchen table with my aunt and uncle and we're having an evening snack. A pot of tea and a slice of toast with homemade rhubarb jam. My aunt has a collection of teapots on a shelf next to the stove. Six of them, various colours and shapes. But the one she uses daily for family, the regular teapot, rests on a ceramic tile in the space between the four burners. The regular one is the one she's using tonight. I've been in this house, at this table, several times, but never alone and able to think somewhat freely.

My uncle is always telling a story, a twinkle in his eye, and my aunt doesn't follow me around like the nuns or my mother and father. I haven't noticed her watching me, but I've only been here one day. I watch because that's what I'm accustomed to doing—watching to see if someone is watching me make a mistake. Someone waiting in ambush.

My uncle is the only one on either side of the family who tells yarns, and he swears all the stories are true. My aunt pretends she's annoyed but I think it's because she's heard them multiple times and with every telling they become more unbelievable.

My uncle applies rhubarb jam to his toast. My aunt pours the tea.

Margaret, my uncle says, *you probably don't know about the Newfoundland man who worked in New York, do you? Very nice fellow.*

I tell him no, I don't.

It frightened the wits right clean out of me, he says. *A few years ago. I was down on the sidewalk and saw the whole thing. The man was working on constructing a skyscraper and he fell right off the top of the building—tripped over a pile of lumber and was headed down to a fast and certain death. As he was speeding towards the ground he remembered that he had a hammer and a large nail in his pocket.* My uncle stirs his tea.

He was a quick-thinking guy. As fast as humanly possible, he pulled that nail from his pocket, grabbed that hammer from his other pocket, and drove the nail into the side of the skyscraper and held on till a rescue crew reached him. He has a store now on the other side of Newfoundland where they sell life-saving hammers and nails—and that's not a word of a lie, he says, and takes a long sip of his tea.

My aunt mutters something under her breath, my uncle winks, and I know enough not to side with either one of them.

We wash the dishes, put things away, and I go upstairs to my room where I've already set out my pyjamas. My aunt will help me set up in the morning, *after we've all had a good night's sleep.*

From the window in my room, the spare room, I can see an enormous wide sky—thousands of stars, the Milky Way, the Big Dipper, and blue moonlight on trees. The outline of roofs. Billowing clouds are racing across the June sky. Shadows from trees make lines on the ground, like a grid. The cool breeze increases. It's the cold wind from the bay. A night bird gives a lone whistle and somewhere off in the distance there's a response. They've finally found one another. At midnight and daybreak there are birds, and every hour in between. Every hour it seems somewhere a bird is singing. Part of the bay is visible, a shining black surface at rest for the night.

In daytime, my mother would see this view as beautiful: a window overlooking mountains and sky, a shimmering bay, a few houses, trees, and gardens below. But if she were standing here alone in the dark, she'd see only horror and hear only frightening noises. She'd recognize nothing. The window and door would be locked and blocked with furniture. She'd miss the sound of the sea, blue light on floorboards, feel of the wind, smell of night air. My mother sees a terrifying, unbelievable picture when she's faced with the night. She'd hear only a storm—any storm. Bending trees. Howling wind. Things knocking against the house. Noise of the clothesline. What I know is out there and what my mother imagines are two worlds apart. I wish I knew how to make a terrified person feel safe. Knew how to calm someone.

With the lamp turned off, blue moonlight is flooding the room. It's spilling over the scrubbed white window ledge, over me in my pyjamas, across the floor and the small hooked rug and the bed. The blue light shines on a branch touching the window. It shines farther away, down the street, next to a neighbour's house.

A small spare room in a hamlet beneath a sky as big as the world. Cool summer breeze on my face. Distant sound of the bay. That's what the picture is. That's how I see it.

Chapter Two

SUNDAY *Day Two*

Sunlight and cool crisp air are flooding the spare room. This is the first day in my life away from my mother's affliction. Away from her debilitating fear of the night. Away from the chaos that is never acknowledged. It's as if each person living inside our house is three different people—how we live inside the house, how we live outside the house, and what we're like just after leaving the house.

Curtains are barely moving. Sky is icy blue with pink across the horizon. Puffy white clouds. The window overlooks fields and a bay. Whitewashed houses and fences. Grass ripples like waves in an ocean. Sheep and lambs on a hill. This is the type of environment people are sent to if they're weak from tuberculosis. Thank God I'm not, but I'm grateful to be in a place where no one is beating something into or out of my head.

Last night, I dreamt everything was reversed. Like writing on paper when held up to a mirror. I couldn't understand anything. It was incomprehensible. Then I woke up, shifted to the other side of the bed, facing the window, and went back to sleep. Everything had righted itself like magic. I could read everything.

It's Sunday so I get dressed in different clothes. Blue cotton dress, good shoes, white socks, a straw hat tied under my chin. The dress goes over my head with three cloth-covered buttons in back and I stretch to reach behind my own shoulders. A flick of my hair with the brush. Secure the ribbon under my chin. Downstairs, and skip breakfast. Sunday morning automatically brings with it fasting.

One Sunday, after church, I was so hungry after twelve hours of fasting—and too hungry to wait for lunch—that I stood in front of the fridge, door opened just enough so I could reach the chicken intended for dinner, and stole a piece of brown, crispy skin. One small crispy piece after another. Without realizing what I was doing, I peeled one entire side of the bird. My mother was well beyond rage—*beyond, beyond!*—and whacked me across the side of the head. But the situation was hopeless. Half the chicken was bald and the skin was inside me.

My aunt is busy with the two boys in the kitchen. A church service on the radio. It's her turn to stay home—she and my uncle take turns.

Well, you're dressed up like a Christmas turkey, my aunt says, and smiles.

I wave. Out the door, down the steps, through the garden, open and close the gate, up the road to the church, up the scrubbed wooden steps, pull the wooden door open and I can smell candle wax. The church is small and impeccably clean. Two stained glass windows: Jesus walking away from the tomb and Mary being crowned in heaven by the Holy Ghost. Air is filled with the remains of incense. Windows are open. A cool breeze and the sound of birds. I'm early—most people arrive at the very last minute.

I genuflect, dip my right hand into a dish being held by a white marble angel, bless myself, slide into a pew, and look up. On the ceiling, surrounded by rose and emerald, a giant golden bird with blazing wings is sailing towards me. The Holy Spirit. A perfect place to pray.

I'm praying almost hourly now—in the morning at home, four times in school, grace before and after each meal, and before going to bed. And that doesn't include Sunday Mass and the holy days of obligation. I'm praying for savages, for all the non-Catholics who will never see heaven, and for babies in limbo—though I'm unclear why since we know they're all doomed.

The sacristy door to the left of the altar is closed. Sacristies all look the same. A small, clean room with cabinets for liturgical items. Crucifix over the door. Candlesticks, cross, a bottle of wine. Smell of incense. Holy books. A rack of vestments—chasubles, albs, elaborate gowns in various colours representing a liturgical season, everything edged with gold. Plain black gowns that altar boys wear and white lacy overgowns. Priests and altar boys enter that room in their regular clothes, then appear on the altar in fancy robes and there's always a different look on their face—serious and unforgiving. But I know they were just in that room changing out of their trousers and shirts, standing around in their underwear—bare legs fully exposed. I could be struck dead for having the thought, with no chance to atone for my sin because I'll be found dead in the pew. Purgatory for several years with the rest of the sinners—it couldn't be hell.

More lights are turned on. People drift in. Two altar boys and a priest enter wearing their robes. I know they were just standing around in their underwear. An altar boy rings a bell. We all make the sign of the cross, and the priest begins to say Mass. Then Latin, a few hymns—"Come, Holy Ghost," "Tantum Ergo"—and we line up for Communion. I receive the Host, return to my seat, let the thin white wafer dissolve on the roof of my mouth, and silently repeat the prayer we're supposed to be saying: *Lord, I am not worthy that you should come under my roof. Say but the word and my soul shall be healed.* I know we're all supposed to be houses of God and that my body is a precious temple—that if I pray for worthiness, God will come under my roof—but when I say the prayer, all I can think of is the roof of my mouth. *I am not worthy that you should come under the roof of my mouth.* The tiny white Host is stuck to the roof of my mouth, and I'm hoping that I'm worthy of having it stuck there. And hoping that nothing is stuck to the soles of my shoes as I kneel at the altar rail with both soles fully exposed to the entire congregation. Worrying about the roof of my mouth and the soles of my shoes makes Communion a moment of complete anxiety every Sunday morning.

After Communion, people reflect, and our thoughts drift like a dory, right out to the bay and beyond.

When my father was growing up in the hamlet, there were only a few Catholic families. Mass was held in a local hotel, the homes of two Catholic families, or right in Pop's store, which is now run by my uncle. Father Finn was the priest. He arrived by train every Sunday, listened to a few people's stories, and set up his church—a cloth-covered table, crucifix and candles, a chalice for wine, something for water, a plate for the Hosts. A church right there in the middle of somebody's living room with the sofa and table lamps, or inside Pop's store, away from the vegetables. That might explain why my father prays every day of his life—his own father's store once served as a church—he'd grown up on an altar.

Father Finn would say Mass and deliver a sermon. The topic might be taking care of the elderly. *Remember yer obligations. Fire and brimstone! The older the fiddler, the sweeter the tune. Take care of yer elderly. The old dog for the hard road. Fire and brimstone! Shoulder to the wheel. Brimstone!* Then he'd give a final blessing. Everyone would say *Thanks be to God,* have tea and something homemade, then goodbye and everyone would go their own way.

People in Newfoundland are always stopping for cups of hot tea and something homemade. No matter what happens in life, a cup of tea is part of the remedy.

The roof just blew off the house!

Sit down, my dear. I'll make a pot of tea and a biscuit.

My mother drinks tea every day of her life and then reads her own leaves. If I see her turn her cup upside down and get a penetrating look on her face, I know something horrific is going to come out of that cup. The possibility of joy never seems to reside in her leaves—only disaster. When she has that penetrating look, I try not to provoke her. I try not to provoke the nuns, but it's hopeless—there's no way to escape provoking a nun. I try not to provoke my father. I spend a good deal of my life trying not to provoke anyone.

My mother's superstitions and rituals have existed through all eleven years of my life. Added to that is the nuns' threatening narrative of damnation and the real possibility of spending eternity in the hot fires of hell with the devil himself. My entire life is filled with a belief in the unverifiable.

Summer, 1952. I'm eight years old. Women in Greece are allowed to vote. The United States explodes an atom bomb in Nevada and it's televised live across the nation. Johnnie Ray and "Walkin' My Baby Back Home." Rosemary Clooney. *Singin' in the Rain.* Canadian troops go to Korea and we're in my father's car and parked in front of Pop's store. My father is at the wheel. My mother asks the woman who's in the back seat with me to read the bumps on my head. The woman could very well be a gypsy. She has dark hair and dark eyes and wears a dark hat with a feather and dark ribbon trim—the sort of hat that old women wear. She holds her purse close to her body.

The tone in my mother's voice seems to imply that there could be an ominous prediction, so be forewarned. I sit straight and alert on the seat. The woman places her hands on my head, rummages through my hair, and roams my scalp with the tips of her fingers, then announces abruptly and loudly, *I can't read her head!*

I have no idea what causes the woman to give up on me, or what's wrong with my head. I don't know what my mother expects to hear from the woman or what she suspects herself. I don't know what's wrong with me. If I have bumps, are they inferior or do they represent something so petrifying that the woman can't bring herself to announce it? She steps out of the car and disappears into the night.

We return to our house with me feeling like a complete and absolute failure, although I'm not sure what I've just failed. I have an unreadable skull. Something else to add to my bent head, slightly pigeon-toed feet, and tragic look on my face. In addition to everything else, I now have an unreadable head—I am possibly bumpless!

An altar boy rings the bell, we sing "Holy God, We Praise Thy Name," the priest gives final benediction, my uncle and everyone else says *Thanks be to God,* and women gather their purses. Altar candles are snuffed and threads of smoke rise to the ceiling. Someone closes the windows. The priest meets everyone at the front door, and some people linger. Then he changes out of his robe and drives away in his car—off to say Mass in another hamlet, a cloud of dust trailing behind, a Saint Christopher medal, patron saint for safe travel, wobbling on his dashboard.

If cavemen lived in Newfoundland, they probably travelled by dinosaur, and since there weren't any roads, they had no need for a medal. The Beothuk travelled by foot and canoe and had their own feathers and charms so they didn't need a Catholic saint. The first explorers in Newfoundland travelled by ship and came here for only one reason: the fish. Since Christopher Columbus was one of the first to arrive, and since he had the same name as the saint, my guess is he had his own medal.

My father doesn't have a Saint Christopher medal. With all the driving he does, you'd think he'd have two—one on each dashboard. At any moment, a moose could leap in front of the car and demolish him. If I mention this, he'll say, *Don't be so foolish!* If I ask a nun a stupid question, she gives me the evil eye. So I don't ask anyone anything.

The church doors are locked. Everyone says *Fair weather to you* or *See you next week.* My uncle and I walk back to the house and that's it until next Sunday morning.

After lunch, my aunt and I set up my room—hang blouses, fill drawers. Good shoes under the bed. The bedroom curtains are white and edged with red. A red geranium on the windowsill. There's a white wooden table with plenty of room for things I've collected already—a stone as flat as a pancake, a glass jar with wildflowers and pieces of fern. Space for my brush and straw hat. And space for my *Webster's Pocket Dictionary*—because I love words. They're like paint chips. Dozens of meanings for a single word.

The bed has a red afghan with flowers and birds. Three enormous round cushions decorate the entire top of the bed, except now I'll have to move them at night and set them up every morning. There's a calendar from the Stokes Seeds company and, because it's June, there's a red rose. The Sacred Heart is in a red plastic frame over the bed. The hooked rug next to the bed is a rectangle with three red roses. Apparently anything red ends up in the spare room. The floorboards are painted white and even though it's late June, the floor gets cold at night. In the middle of winter, this floor would be in desperate need of hooked rugs.

Hooked rugs are made from pieces of old clothes and curtains—nothing is wasted. The final stage in the life of a shirt is often its place in a rug. Backings can come from brin bags, washed and then sewn together. In the early Newfoundland days, patterns were drawn with soot from the stove and the end of a stick served as a pencil.

There's a bureau—white with red wooden knobs. A drawing of flowers above it. The lamp on the bureau is white.

That's the spare room: a bed and a hooked rug; a table, bureau, and lamp; a calendar; the Sacred Heart; and a drawing. And for some reason, I feel especially small here. Not in a bad way. I feel as if there's room for me here with plenty of space left over. That there's space all around me—as if there's room for everything in the world, including myself.

It's seven thirty. The boys have gone to bed early, supper dishes are washed, and the evening is warm. I'm tired, but it's not a bad kind of tired. Moths are spinning around the outdoor overhead light bulb. I can see them through the screen door.

My uncle is sitting at the cleared kitchen table, one arm over the back of his chair, the other hand holding his cigar. He stares out the window—maybe thinking about the store or the family. There's no way to tell. The curtains move slowly—just enough to know there's a breeze. My aunt is reading a magazine in the living room. The house is quiet. Very quiet.

I can do whatever I want for a while. Walk by myself. Maybe take a different direction. Walk by the water—it's only ten minutes away. Everything is only ten minutes away, in every direction. *Just a gunshot away.* I'd walk beside water every day of my life if I could.

Rocks are still warm from the heat of the sun. A beautiful dusty rose and dusty blue sky and one white cloud, a small puff, as if someone left it behind. The waves are silver wrinkles floating on black. A dog barks—a single *woof.*

So here I am, between grade six and grade seven, wind and mist on my face, in a hamlet with a spare-room window overlooking a bay.

I'll be taking care of the two boys for a few hours each day and it makes me feel different. It's my very first chance to live somewhere else for a while. Away from the nuns and my mother's affliction. Especially my mother's affliction. There's no telling what to expect from one day to the next. She lives in a world of superstition and terror and so, by extension, do we. She uses tea leaves and omens and cards and the assistance of a woman who can read bumps on a head, if the head has any bumps worth reading.

There are days when I'll come home after school, and she'll be upstairs on the bed, shoes and nylons thrown on the floor, body stiff like a plank, and she'll tell me to rub her feet. Her feet are hard and calloused and I think pain escapes when I touch them. She pays me ten cents a foot.

I stay on the shore with the stillness and sunset. New places to walk. Waves crashing on rocks. Rumbling sounds. Seaweed tangled on shells. Grey boulders and pebbles. A Newfoundland evening.

Newfoundland is triangular, with unpredictable winters and sometimes violent winds. The west coast is an extension of North America. The east coast was once part of Africa. The continents collided, lava gushed forth, and Newfoundland was created—and with it a soil combination producing flowers found nowhere else on the face of the earth. The island is covered with mountains 300 million years old. This is exactly where I was born eleven years ago—on a 300-million-year-old triangle.

I return to the house, past houses with people settling in for the evening. The boys are muttering in their sleep and the wind is increasing—it moves the curtains and geranium leaves.

From the window, I can see two moths spinning around the backdoor light bulb. They twirl and dip around the dangerous warmth. They've been there all evening.

I've only received one prize in my life—best poster in the town library poster contest. The library is located directly above the town bowling alley, and except for the roars from an occasional strike, and bowling pins crashing, the place is relaxing.

I drew a hobo with a sack attached to a stick, which he held over his shoulder. The sack was filled with an assortment of books, and he was smiling. I glued a piece of real pussy willow on top of his cap and I won, and the prize was a book called *The Lives of Moths and Butterflies.*

The body of a moth has thirteen sections connected by joints so it can move in any direction. When a moth is first born, its wings are crumpled, and it's long and flabby and looks like a worm. It can be easily caught, so it has to move quickly—do anything—*Move, move, move, you look like a worm!*

Moths start out in life completely traumatized. They frantically race from their cocoon to the nearest branch, hang themselves upside down, and let their crushed wings fan out. They look like wrinkled, upside-down angels. When their wings are straightened and smooth, the moths flit away as if they've been flying for years, and there they are downstairs around the light bulb over the kitchen door.

As the lights fade in each hamlet house, the world outside turns ebony black.

Flowers in my aunt's garden are almost invisible. The light over the back door is turned off and the moths will navigate by stars and the moon.

The world is a black-and-white painting with silver and blue. A hamlet in shadows. A *Dazzling White* moon in a *Midnight Blue* sky. A white sequin on velvet. Blue moonlight on ebony water. The wind is quiet. And if wind has a colour, its colour is *Sterling Silver.* My father's paint chips up in the sky, as seen from a spare-room window.

Pray, bed, sleep.

Chapter Three

MONDAY *Day Three*

My aunt is talking to the two boys and my uncle downstairs. Smell of toast, frying eggs, and a commercial for Chock full o'Nuts on the radio. Teresa Brewer and "A Sweet Old Fashioned Girl."

Make the bed. Pray. Look out the window. Because so much of the hamlet is whitewashed, with the sun hitting it, everything is brilliant white, like enamel. If the morning sun is a paint chip, it's *Enamel.* The bay is a blanket of silver tinsel.

A few people are out in their gardens, weeding and raking, and seagulls are gliding like pieces of floating white paper.

Sound of the morning news. More trouble with the Suez Canal. News from the fisheries. Factory trawlers from Europe and Russia and Asia. Gigantic nets catching fish twenty-four hours a day in all kinds of weather. News about salmon and cod. "The Yellow Rose of Texas."

I dreamt about flowers last night. A man gave me an empty seed package. He told me to plant the picture of the flowers on the front of the package.

Down the stairs. Into the kitchen. My uncle is finishing breakfast and the two boys are examining food. My aunt stands by the stove. I slide onto my chair and she puts a plate in front of me—egg, ham, a slice of buttered toast. She makes her own breakfast and is the last one to eat. My uncle makes a fast sign of the cross, pushes his chair from the table, says *I'll see you by and by,* and he's gone.

Clean up. Out the door, down the steps, into the yard, make sure the gate is closed. Push the two boys on a garden swing, make up a few stories about the Beothuk, and play in the yard.

Children are running and yelling or racing their bicycles. Sound of phones and cars and clothesline pulleys.

At home, the shops are all open by now. My father is making deliveries of cookies and paint. My mother is out in the garden until darkness swallows the sun, which it will.

I don't know why my mother feels safe in the garden. Outside, she's calm and relaxed, watering peony roots or planting spring bulbs. Cutting back foliage. But inside the house, she's twelve different people. She's one woman in town and another at home. In her own way, *street angel, house devil.* She's lonely, frightened, demanding, violent, and superstitious. And Presbyterian. This type of person needs rest and my mother doesn't rest. Or can't. She's like an iceberg out in the bay. What's beneath the surface is a large, floating mystery. But my father is home and I'm in the hamlet saying *Good,* when people ask *How are ye gettin' on, my dear?* Because I am.

Noon.

Into the house. Lunch. Clean up and out the door again. Walk around the hamlet with my aunt and the two boys. The ground is soft—there's not as much concrete here.

We visit my uncle's store. Shelves with every imaginable kind of grocery. Upstairs, the windows are covered with thick yellow plastic blocking the sun. Racks of dimly lit clothing and boxes with buttons and trim—a world of ribbons and lace and long bolts of fabric. Ladies hats next to a mirror—a display of elegant severed heads. That's what my mother would see. Wherever I look I see the affliction. It's like feeling the strap even when I'm not being strapped.

Off to itself, high off the floor, a collection of knives in a locked glass case. Hunting knives in brown leather sheaths. Knives for moose and caribou season. Knives for cleaning fish. Small, gift-boxed pocket knives. Kitchen knives—long, silver blades with thick, black handles, and a sign: *Make your cutting more enjoyable.*

It's the very end of grade two. An early rainy morning, before leaving for school. I say something to my mother. We're both in the kitchen and she's chopping something near the sink. My father is waiting outside in the car to take me to school. I say something. I can't remember what—it's completely gone from my mind—but I say something and she raises the butcher knife high in the air and lunges towards me and I run for my life, through the kitchen, through the hall, out the door, through the yard, out the gate, across the street, and into the car.

Mom just chased me with the butcher knife!

Oh, she's only joking.

He turns the key in the ignition, hits the gas, up the road, around the corner, up the hill, stop in front of the school. Into the furnace room in an orderly fashion. Sit at my desk in an orderly fashion. Face the nun.

We move away from the knives and look at the severed heads for a while. Then down the stairs and goodbye to the people behind the counter.

See you by and by.

Yes, my dear.

Out the door, up the street, visit people along the way.

Hello, my dear. How are ya? a woman asks my aunt.

Best kind, my dear. Couldn't be better. And they talk for a while.

Bring the boys home. My aunt makes supper. Pray, eat, pray. There's no end to the praying. She washes the dishes. I dry. We put things away slowly. My father would be finished in half the time. My father does everything fast. He walks fast. Talks fast. He clears the table fast. If you take your eyes off your plate it's gone. He even prays fast. I gave him an eight-week novena one year. A prayer to Saint Anthony every Thursday for eight weeks. He read it all in one day, start to finish. He wanted to get it done. My father lives with the goal of staying one step ahead of disaster.

Evening news on the radio. Joey Smallwood's new idea: move hundreds of families from small Newfoundland outports and put them all together in a few large villages. Joey Smallwood is Newfoundland's premier, but everyone just calls him Joey. News of the world: trouble with the Suez Canal—there's no end to the trouble with the Suez Canal. More trouble in Hungary. Report from the fishery: price of fresh cod—gutted, head-on. Time of the morning tide. A Newfoundland folk song—"Harbour Le Cou." Tuesday's weather report. Songs by the Happy Valley Gang.

The boys go to bed and I walk down to the bay by myself. A man is out for a stroll. He nods and tips his cap.

So, you're babysitting the two boys for a while.

Everyone knows who I am and what I'm doing.

Yes.

How's it going?

Good.

Are they giving you any trouble, my dear?

I tell him no trouble.

Stay on your toes with those young ones. You know what they say about children—steal the eyes out of your head and come back for the sockets. Stay on your toes now?

I tell him I'll stay on my toes, then walk towards a path that follows the shoreline. Wildflowers and smell of salt water. Fireflies flit about, then collapse on the ground like sparks. A church bell rings. It's either Catholic or non-Catholic—they all sound the same when you can't see them.

Waves lap against rocks, then out to the sea, then back to the rocks. Gulls dip and soar. Wind blows over my body. Clouds roll across the sky. Branches are bending and creaking. Everything around me is moving. It's a miracle I'm keeping my balance.

The path is covered with shadows and leafy patterns. A clean fresh wind, sky changing to dusk, smell of salt water, and sounds from the bay. I'm exactly where I've always wanted to be. Alone, with no one around me. Quiet and space. No one on top of me.

Three wooden benches are shaded by branches—a perfect shelter if you were walking here during the rain. And behind them, concealed beneath trees, a tiny, abandoned stone chapel. Like a picture torn from a storybook. The ground is a tangle of overgrown thistle and weeds. Vine-covered windows. An angel is carved in stone above the door.

The door is unlocked. It has only a black metal handle. When we lived in the woods, in a cabin, the storeroom had the same exact handle, right down to the colour. Hard-backed beetles lived in the walls. My mother wouldn't enter the room. *Get the vegetables, Margaret.* I held the saucepan in front like a sword, kicked the storeroom door open like Rory Calhoun, grabbed the vegetables, and ran like a bandit.

The chapel is furnished, dirty, and dark. Cobwebs in every corner. Layers of dust on the floor. A water-stained altar with a dusty crucifix in the centre. Dusty kneelers with worn red cushions. Fat wasps are buzzing outside the window. Baskets of smooth, flat pebbles line a shelf. This may be a Catholic chapel, and taking a stone may be a sin, but I pocket a tiny one anyway. The smaller the stone, the smaller the crime.

I turn around and a woman in a long blue dress is reaching towards me. My heart completely stops beating. I should never be in here. I force my eyes to adjust to the light and I can see the Virgin Mary and she's staring straight at me. It could be a miracle but the floor is so dirty I'm afraid to fall to my knees. Her dress has a rip in the front and both eyes are chipped. It's a life-sized statue of the Blessed Virgin abandoned behind the door, but now my heart won't stop pounding or start beating—I'm not sure which. Everything here was abandoned, including Mary. This is exactly what happened to us.

It's 1952, the end of summer, and my father's business collapses. I'm eight years old. It's after the furnace room, after finding out I have an unreadable skull, and after Sandy's apparent suicide.

My father's business collapses and he loses his store and our house and all our belongings and we move to the woods, forty miles up the highway. No neighbours, means of communication, electricity, water, or heat. Only a structure my father builds with what seems like a hammer, a saw, and a large box of nails. A spot in the woods is a bathroom. Perishables live in a brook with a family of ducks.

My mother cooks on a Coleman camp stove—two burners and regular flare-ups. Blue flames leap to the ceiling. My father comes home and the Coleman is hanging from tree limbs. Flung through the door and into the woods—a fiery ball headed straight for the forest. It's a miracle she doesn't set the country on fire. My father pieces the Coleman together and we eat in absolute silence. It's like being in school with the nuns except my mother isn't wearing a uniform and no one is ringing a bell.

There's a metal tub and a scrub board and my mother's hands get wrinkled from water and her knuckles are bleeding and raw. It's a terrible time and terrifying that we have to live this way. That we lost the store, our house, and all our possessions. That my mother's knuckles are bleeding and raw. That we have to leave everything and live in the woods—but we do.

Water flows from the earth outward, through rivers and lakes and into the mouth of the ocean. There's water at Lourdes and Fátima. Water is everywhere except down by the cabin.

We find a spring on the other side of the highway, a quarter mile from the cabin. We walk to the highway. My mother carries two buckets and I carry one. We cross the Trans-Canada, ease our way under a barbed wire fence, and cross a field to a spring with the coldest water I've ever touched in my life. Fill the three buckets, re-cross the field, under the wire, re-cross the highway, back to the cabin. Try not to spill a drop.

This is how the Beothuk lived until they were tragically killed by the settlers. They built wigwams and cone-shaped wooden houses. Fished for salmon and got their water from a river or stream. Hunted caribou in the winter. Dried and stored their own meat. Made their own clothes. Endured brutal winters and storms, built canoes, and travelled along the Newfoundland coast. But we arrive to the wilderness by way of my father's blue Chevrolet, along the Trans-Canada Highway, and without a Saint Christopher medal.

A man comes to the cabin and circles our yard for most of the day. He walks with a branch held in front, and the branch leads to an underground stream, and a well is dug and water is struck like gold. We have our own clear running water.

Between the loss of our home, the move to the woods, the loss of neighbours, electricity, water, and heat, and the complete darkness and demons, my mother may have been going insane. I don't know what she was thinking when my father was gone. She walked sometimes in the evening, with her winter coat over her nightgown. Her silhouette a combination of shadows. She felt safer outdoors.

Outdoors, I can run up the road, away from the danger.

Inside, she was trapped by the walls.

My father travels the outport roads selling cookies and paint, my mother walks outdoors in her nightgown because there are too many demons inside the cabin, and I'm in school with the nuns—on my knees, praying ten times a day. At night, I have a recurring silent nightmare. I'm being captured by strangers who are always on horseback outside the storeroom. I'll run through the cabin to the front door, but there'll be more strangers—tall, on horseback, waiting. Like a scene from a western, but there's never a hero.

Getting to school from the woods when my father's away, which is often, requires catching a ride in Mr. Clark's egg truck. Mr. Clark and his wife have a chicken farm a few miles from the cabin.

Mrs. Clark irons her curtains so they're spectacularly beautiful and Mr. Clark packs only eggs that are flawless because his customers want perfection. Every morning, we drive into town with a truck carefully packed with cartons of perfect eggs and I tell him about my homework or what I saw in the woods and he responds with the same exact phrase: *Well, by the hole in my coat!* He can't believe all the things that I know. *Well by the hole in my coat, Margaret.*

I arrive in town around seven o'clock, stay with non-Catholic relatives, then walk to school at the appropriate time. If it's raining, I pray to Jesus and Mary that my book bag is water repellent—otherwise it's the strap.

After school, I stay with the same non-Catholic relatives, then get a ride back with Mr. Clark in the truck, which is now empty, or with my father if he's in town.

My uncle is the only one home after school, so he's in charge of me. The second I arrive at the front door, he hands me two quarters—forty cents for the 4:15 p.m. movie, and ten cents for candy. Five movies a week.

I'm in love with the movies. Detectives and outer space. Bing Crosby and Doris Day. Heroes and villains. The hero sweeps the woman to safety just seconds before the train rolls over her glove, which she left on the track. Tragic movies about the Depression—soup kitchens with bowls and cups in the hundreds. Potatoes and gravy for hundreds, and some people have doubles. Then a miracle happens. Some people are rescued and it has an ending so sad I don't want the lights to come up because I've got tears streaming down both sides of my face and a lump in my throat so big I can't speak.

The Great Caruso. Some of the nuns went to see that one—I saw them way in the back, in the dark.

And the westerns. Gene Autry or Roy Rogers. He'll be riding on a beautiful horse and he's wearing a white hat and singing about wide open fields. And music is coming from out of the sky and Gabby Hayes is right by his side and singing along. Then a band of cowboys shows up and they're all wearing black hats and they're all on black horses. And Gene Autry or Roy Rogers stops singing. And Gabby Hayes starts to worry. Then they show up at a saloon and there's a terrible fight—tables and chairs go flying. The bartender ducks behind a counter and comes back with a gun. Everybody grabs a gun, and Gene Autry or Roy Rogers shoots with a gun in each hand and kills everyone who's wearing a black hat. Then Gene Autry or Roy Rogers will ride out of town on his beautiful horse, wearing his spotless white hat, and there won't be a speck of dust on his shirt and he'll be singing "Back in the Saddle Again" and his horse will be smiling and Gabby Hayes will be smiling and music will be in the air. It's all perfect. I never want to go home. I want to ride into our town with Gene Autry or Roy Rogers and wave to the neighbours and I'll be wearing a white hat and white cowgirl dress and music will be playing all over town. Gene Autry or Roy Rogers will be singing and everyone in town will be smiling.

After the movies, either Mr. Clark or my father picks me up, and we ride back to the cabin—my head filled with stories of Hollywood. Pray, supper, pray. Homework, pray, sleep. Up again.

On the weekends, I build my own forts with rocks and pieces of logs. I listen to wind, just like the Beothuk. I can think anything. No one is banging something into my brain or banging me up because it's not in my brain yet. There's only the perfume of pine and phlox. Only round pieces of tree stump. Smell of safety. The whole world should be inside this fort.

It's the middle of winter. Late afternoon. As Mr. Clark and I approach the cabin, we see an enormous white camel standing in the front yard. It's half as tall as the cabin. My mother built a gargantuan camel inside the fence. An enormous snow camel with a white frozen hump in the middle of Newfoundland's frozen forest.

I come home in the egg truck, ride a white frozen camel beneath spruce trees laden with snow, see the affliction, memorize something in Latin, then bed and up again. Pray, breakfast, pray.

During the winter, I practice the life of a missionary and crawl on my hands and knees through snowdrifts, forging paths where before there were none, jacket zippered against the frost. I don't go inside until the knees of my snow pants are frozen with snow and my mind and body are freezing and I can't see anymore in the dark. Endurance. What I need. And talking to something invisible—like the missionaries praying to Jesus while they forged a path to the savages, or the saints on their way to a tribe of barbarians, bringing the gospel.

My mother sees demons and swears. The nuns strap us and tell us to get on our knees and ask for forgiveness. My father is strict and recites the rosary and I crawl on my knees through the snow, bringing the gospel to African savages.

1953 is over. It's 1954 and we're still in the woods. Grade four. I'm nine years old. Books about the geological features of earth—glacial erosion and minerals in distant countries. Books about rare Newfoundland flowers. About the little African boy with his grass hut beneath tropical trees. About the girl who lives in an igloo. About people in wigwams. There's no mention of people who build cabins deep in the woods after they've lost their store and all their belongings and ride into school in an egg truck and ride a frozen camel in the Newfoundland woods and pray on their knees six times a day minimum—eight times a day, ten times a day.

It's a wonder my mother survives the cabin. It's a wonder anyone does. After two years, we move back into town.

My father may have obtained the new house at a discount because he took the owner's son with the structure. My father took every lamp, bureau, and armchair, the kitchen table and chairs, the electric range, and the owner's son—a quiet man at the table every morning and evening for several months until he found a place of his own.

The biggest difference between the house in town and the cabin is the factor of light. Because the house is right in the middle of town, there's an absence of forest. The front yard has two poplar trees exceeding the roof—one on each side of the gate. There's a heavy wire fence and a hedge high enough to fully conceal the green wire. If a dog tries to bolt through the hedge it could get a concussion.

The house has a washing machine and for the first time in two years my mother's knuckles aren't bleeding and raw. We have a phone. A radio on a corner shelf in the kitchen. Morning reports from the fishery department—news about capelin. Music by The Royal Canadians and Nat King Cole. *Name the Newfoundlander. The Hank Snow Serenade* on Saturday night. Patti Page. Commercials for laundry detergent with dessert plates inside. *The Hour of St. Francis.* On Sundays, classical music and *The Bing Crosby Show.* Margot Davies and her broadcast from England—*Hello Newfoundland, this is Margot Davies calling from the BBC, London*—as she delivers news about Newfoundland people overseas. Her voice is refined and perfect and she speaks for hours and never makes a mistake. I want to be like that someday.

One of the kitchen windows overlooks a neighbour's garden. A painting in perpetual bloom. As if they'd removed a masterpiece from the wall of a foreign museum and wished it to life in their Newfoundland yard. Rows of nasturtium on each side of the walkway. Blue morning glories and pansies. Primrose and phlox run the length of the yard. Violets and shells ring fruit trees. Rose bushes are planted on their side of the fence. My chair faces the stove, my back to their garden. I know this view exists behind me with its richness and colours—I catch a glimpse as I slide onto my chair. But I observe their garden through the eyes in the back of my head. I can see it whenever I close my eyes. Behind me. Dahlias, lilacs, and roses—their perfume drifting in through our kitchen window. Everything but their fragrance is fenced.

After the move into town, we use the cabin on weekends. I forget my homework one weekend and my father gets in the car and drives up the highway in the darkness of night. He understands the terror of nuns. Was taught by the Christian Brothers. Saw young boys slammed against lockers.

I lie in bed in the dark and hear my mother enter my room. I feel her lean over me, hear her breathing. I think she's going to kiss me good night.

If anything happens to your father on that road, I'll kill you.

I know she means it. But if I arrive in school without homework, the nuns will kill me. Either way, there's a very good chance that I'll be dead in the morning.

My mother is thirty-six years old when we move back into town. But there'd been too many fears up the highway. Too many demons inside the rooms, outside the door. Monsters hiding deep in the woods. Too much coldness—frost on the inside of windows. Too many shadows. Too much loneliness. Loneliness can manifest itself in any number of ways. I think it changed her forever.

I pull the chapel door shut, fasten the black metal handle, and stand outside in the stillness. There's no one on this path except me. A dog in the hamlet barks softly. The sun falls through the horizon—a deep red-orange sun sliced in half with a lavender cloud. On the way back to the house, sounds of the bay and a flurry of flowers.

Everything in the spare room is exactly as it was when I left it this morning. The red afghan is smooth across the bed. Three fat cushions are in need of perpetual moving. My pyjamas are still under the pillow. Nothing changed except the view from the window. Sky changes and light changes and the wind moves things. People move things in their gardens. Clothes are put on the line to get an airing during the night, or brought in at the end of the day. The view is never exactly the same. Racket of gulls. Clouds changing colour. Rustle of leaves. Serenade of the sparrows. An ever-changing Newfoundland sky. I want to keep all the images inside my mind, rewind them at will—images seen through a spare-room window. A sky peppered with stars.

My uncle is downstairs puffing on his cigar, turning the pages of the evening paper, and clearing his throat. The two boys are sleeping. The man who told me to watch out that someone didn't come back to steal my eye sockets after stealing my eyes is hopefully resting. My father is watching over my mother, my aunt is setting the table for breakfast, and I'm upstairs, watching a night sky, dark as pitch, through a spare-room window. Sound of crickets. Everyone is busy doing something.

Chapter Four

TUESDAY *Day Four*

By now I'm aware of my aunt and uncle's routine. They get up first. He has a wash and a shave. She makes breakfast. Smell of toast and frying eggs. Clink of dishes. I get up next, and she makes my breakfast. My uncle leaves. The two boys get up. I make their toast, eggs, and juice, say *Down the chute* two or three times, and the day unfolds. Then a walk by myself in the evening. Talk with new people.

How's yerself, my dear?

Good.

Turn a corner.

How's she cutting, my dear?

Good.

Turn another corner.

How are ye gettin' on, my dear?

Good.

Back to the house.

Last night, I dreamt submarines were crashing through houses. The town in my dream was flooded and everyone had a tent except I had to share mine with my mother and father, so I decided to sit outside and read. I got to page fourteen and then went for a walk. Nuns were cooking and selling food on what remained of the beach. Waves were coming in fast. Water covered the people. I saw myself being carried away by the storm but I felt it was better to stay on land so I wished myself out of the water. Now that I'm awake, I don't know if anyone else survived.

A breeze is moving the curtains, sunlight is making everything gold, and the bay is shimmering. Gulls are making their morning racket. In Newfoundland, you can learn a lot about life from the gulls. If a man has a big appetite, he eats like a gull. If he sits off by himself and looks lonely, he's as lonesome as a gull on a rock. If gulls fly high, stormy weather is near.

I can hear people outside on the road.

How are ye gettin' on, b'y?

Can't complain, b'y. Can't complain. How's yerself?

Can't complain.

Make the bed. Move the cushions. Pray, wash, dress. I still pray in the spare room, even though no one would know. It's a habit. I'll probably pray till I die. If I'm not thinking about anything else, I'm praying. But it feels more relaxed when I pray on my own. Plus, there's a very good chance that I'll go straight to hell if I don't.

This is the first full day in my life when I'll be in charge of anything and I'm not sure how I'm supposed to be feeling. Flick my hair. Down the stairs, into the kitchen, hello to my aunt. My uncle is already on his way to the store.

Smell of toast. Morning news on the radio. Trouble in Poland. Trouble in Hungary. A change in the price of capelin. Two reports about fishing. In Newfoundland, people always talk about salmon and cod. Time of the evening tide. The very best time for fishing is around the time of the tide—both morning and evening. A commercial for Red Rose Tea. A song by Eddy Arnold. More news, except it's the original news from a few minutes ago repeated as if it's all new and nobody noticed. The bulletin board. "How Much Is That Doggie in the Window?" The bulletin board in case we missed it the first time. Johnny Cash.

I make breakfast for the two boys—soft-boiled egg, half slice of buttered toast without crusts, and a half cup of Del Monte orange juice without a trace of cod-liver oil. Not like the orange juice at home in the winter.

Every winter, the Newfoundland government sends free bottles of cod-liver oil to every child's home—ever since the Depression, when we were all destitute. The Depression is over but cod-liver oil continues to flow. My mother tries to conceal it in Del Monte orange juice, but it floats to the top and shimmers. It smells like the raw insides of a cod, and it rolls down my throat where the cod resides for most of the winter. And if the dead fish doesn't prevent me from getting a cold, she makes a concoction with kerosene and blackstrap molasses. Kerosene evokes memories of the Coleman stove in the cabin. I might erupt in blue flames and have to be flung from the house, across the street, and into the neighbour's yard, blazing.

My aunt pours tea and offers more toast. *What tea and toast can't cure, there's no cure for, my dear,* she says and she winks.

She says it's relaxing and adds more milk to her cup.

There's something about her kitchen that's calming and reassuring. It's not the pictures of saints—I see enough of them every day of my life. It's just that when I leave in the morning, I know there's a very good chance that the kitchen will still be here at the end of the day.

I'm nine years old. It's after the move back into town and after Freddie, the boarder, left to find a place of his own. It's around six o'clock in the evening. I'm in the kitchen and my father is especially tense. When he's especially tense, he drums the fingers of his right hand on a table, as if he were playing a five-key piano. And right now, he's drumming.

Every chair, table, lamp, bookcase, and picture—every moveable item—has been moved from one part of the house to another. My mother relocated every item downstairs while my father was selling cookies and paint and I was on my knees with the nuns. It's like a haunted-house movie—a ghost flew through the air and rooms rearranged themselves. My mother has the penetrating look on her face. It's almost a challenge. In addition to everything else, my mother is stubborn.

I don't know how my mother accomplished this in eight hours, or why. There's no sign of a struggle. She simply erased the original rooms—an Etch A Sketch house. Nobody speaks. We just walk through the house looking for furniture.

My aunt puts the top on the jam jar and I finish my tea and toast but I don't notice anything different.

Wash up, out the door, down the steps, through the yard, through the gate, and down the road that leads directly to the wide open field.

A woman is walking around the side of her house and waves us into the yard—that old-fashioned, friendly *Come on in* sort of wave—so I stop by the gate. Her apron pockets are filled with clothespins and she has a piece of lace over her arm—something has dried enough for ironing.

When we lived in the cabin, the clothes dried beautifully on a line tied between trees. The arm of a shirt grabbed the string of an apron and they waltzed with the wind. Everything smelled of flowers and forest. But in winter, everything froze. Blouses and pants hung from the line like parts of anatomy after a hanging or a beheading. They drooped, then froze in place. The arm of a shirt flung itself around the shirt's neck and stayed there. A pant leg bent at the knee and froze—a mid-air genuflection. My mother brought the body parts in at the end of the day, propped them against a chair or on a thin line, and the frozen bits of anatomy talked to themselves in the kitchen during the night, then melted on paper.

The woman dries her hands on her apron, unlatches the gate, and smiles. She has dark brown hair and *River Blue* eyes.

It's a good day on clothes, my dear. 'Ow are ye gettin' on? I 'ear you're babysitting the boys. Are they treating you well, Margaret? No trouble, are they?

No. They're good as gold.

That three-year-old is going to be an 'eartbreaker, my dear. E'd break the 'eart of a grindstone.

She tells me her name is Matilda. I don't ask if she's Waltzing Matilda, but the thought is stuck in my mind and now I can't stop thinking it. She moved here from an outport way down the coast. Eighty-five people, and they didn't have roads—they travelled by boat. She knows my aunt and uncle by their first names, how old the boys are, and what I'm doing here in the hamlet. She knows my name and she knew everyone's name in the outport. She says having the stores in the hamlet is something completely beyond her experience. Her husband is a fisherman and an expert handyman. *That man can fix or build anything, my dear. Give 'im a ball of steel wool and 'e'll knit you a bicycle.*

But Newfoundland was built on the fishery and the fishing industry changed. *And not for the better, my dear.*

Hundreds of factory trawlers from all over the world are fishing right off the Newfoundland shore. They take everything. Just like the explorers.

My dear, if you go out to the cape, you can see them at night, dragging the water—'undreds of factory boats lit up like a city out in the sea. They throw out nets, my dear, the size of three 'ouses, and take everything, even the mother fish. They're working twenty-four hours a day. Replacing all the schooners. Taking the livelihood away from 'undreds of families. People 'ad to walk away from their 'omes and move in with relatives. They 'ad no way to survive, my dear. They 'ad nothing but 'ard bread and scrunchions. They 'ad to leave 'omes that were in their family for three generations. Some left their pictures on walls so strangers would know they once lived there. Some left their Bibles. You know, my dear, those people all left their 'earts.

Winters were harsh for people who stayed.

When times are good, people don't notice the 'ard weather as much. They don't notice that. My 'usband is a courageous man, but 'e wants to look to the future now. 'E was offered a job in the 'amlet, so we pulled up our roots and 'ere we are now, and 'e can still do a bit of fishing. Life in the 'amlet is a different world, my dear, with all the buildings and lights and stores. But that man will never lose 'is love of the sea. 'E's wrung more water out of 'is mitts than most people 'ave sailed over.

She says the boys and I can stop by anytime. *Margaret, my dear, the three of you are as welcome as the angels in 'eaven.*

She says I'll be wonderful with the two boys. I tell her I'm not sure. This is the first time in my life that I've been in charge of anything.

That's what first attempts are for, my dear. They're for learning. See you on the way back.

I don't know if Matilda is a Catholic or if she'd ever consider becoming a nun. She could be a Presbyterian, which would make it completely impossible. But we needed someone like her at the start of grade four. Instead, we got the most evil nun that ever walked on the face of the earth and there's no doubt in my mind about that. Sister Mary Saint Genesius. Never a saint, always a devil.

It's 1954. I'm still in grade four. Marilyn Bell swims Lake Ontario. The Korean War has been over for months and Marilyn Monroe is married to Joe DiMaggio. *I Love Lucy. The Adventures of Ozzie and Harriet.* The Third World is defined: the United States and the West are first, the Soviet Union is second, and everywhere else is third. *Gillette Cavalcade of Sports* and *Candid Camera.* Joey Smallwood—hardly a day goes by when Joey Smallwood isn't in the news. The very first subway in Canada is in Toronto. Bill Haley and rock and roll. Brylcreem commercials.

We have books about landlords and serfs, geography, nature, and pirates in Newfoundland fjords. Questions in Latin on the blackboard, maps of Canada and the rest of the world on the wall, and the girl being beaten in front of the room was born with the sin of dropping her *h*'s but Genesius intends to beat the sin out of her.

Faith, hope, and love. Say it again. Her eyes are bulging and there's a leather strap in her hand.

Faith, 'ope, and love.

SLAP!

Hope! Say it again! Say it again!

No one wants to look, but we're forbidden to close our eyes. There are windows, but we aren't allowed to look through them.

In church, the nuns are a vision of piety. Street angels, house devils.

We fall to our knees and pray to the Virgin Mary. *Virgin most merciful. Mystical rose. Morning star. Queen of peace. Comforter of the afflicted.* Each phrase followed by *Pray for us* in loud, clear voices, like we mean it—and we do. *Pray for us!*

We're told to roll up our sleeves and extend our arms forward, palms up.

The impact makes blisters, like burns from an iron. If we pull our arms back, we're strapped harder. If we cry, we're strapped more, so we learn not to cry. One nun tells me, *Suffering means you'll have more jewels in your crown in heaven.* I can just imagine that crown, heavy with emeralds and pearls. A big diamond right in the centre. I won't ever wear it. I'll give it to a Newfoundland girl in limbo.

The nuns slap girls across the face and then we pray for forgiveness—except the girl who keeps dropping her *h*'s. Jesus will never forgive her. She might as well drop out of school, forget about homework, and go straight to hell.

Say it again!

Faith, 'ope, and—

SLAP! SLAP! Thick leather strap hitting both hands.

We pray the rosary. Three sections: Joyful, Sorrowful, and Glorious. Sorrow reminds me of red—images of blood and martyrs. I have a gushing nosebleed one day after school. I let the red drops fall into a jar, then fasten the lid and put the jar of blood on a shelf in my closet. I have absolutely no idea why I'm saving my blood. My mother finds it and throws it away, but it completely scares the bejesus out of her. In grade four, I was saving my blood—just in case.

Matilda waves goodbye from the gate and the two boys wave back. Down to the field, open the blanket, watch the birds and the view. The Beothuk were probably sitting right here in the field two hundred years ago. Having a meal, keeping an eye on their fire, or watching a canoe in the bay.

I've never been on a boat or a ship in my life. Maybe someday I will. Maybe someone will say, *Would you like to go on a ship, my dear?* And I'll say *Yes, I would.* And I'll look up and it will be Gene Autry—except he'll own a schooner, and we'll sail on the ocean and visit the tropics and there'll be a Saint Christopher medal on board just in case there's a storm. Then back to the hamlet, and I'll say a prayer in thanksgiving for a safe ocean journey. And Gene Autry will pray in thanksgiving.

I talk to the boys all morning, make up a few stories, and watch their every move—I don't want any surprises. I'm not good at conversations, but I tell stories and point things out, and so far it's working. The two-year-old asks *Why?* followed by any number of whys. The three-year-old watches everything.

Look at the crows! And I sing them the crow song. *One for sorrow, two for joy, three for a letter, four for a boy, five for silver, six for gold, seven for a secret that must never be told.*

I try to be calm. Not on edge, which is where I am most of my life. On the edge of a chair, ready for liftoff—away from the nuns and my mother's affliction. Blast off in the kitchen from a piece of linoleum furniture.

My father is always on edge. He doesn't smile often, but he did in old photographs, just as my mother smiled in the black-and-white snapshots. Pictures of fishing trips—my father and men in a boat or posing beside tents and a fire. A kettle boiling with water, tin cups in their hands. High rubber boots. Fishing poles at the ready. A bottle nearby—rum for the end of the day. Supper on tin plates around a crackling fire. He seemed carefree and happy. Now, he seems worried every day of his life. He worries about making sales of cookies and paint.

My mother worries about demons crashing right through the windows or climbing down from the roof or up through the floorboards, and I worry about the nuns and my mother's affliction, my slightly pigeon-toed feet, and whether or not I have normal bumps on my head. If you happen to live in our house, you worry.

The only person I know who doesn't have any worries is Miss Mary Cobb, and I don't know how she does it, year after year. Mary Cobb is my grandmother's sister—my mother's aunt—and she lives alone in the forest, without electricity or even a road. My mother would die of affliction.

Mary Cobb was born nine hundred years after the Vikings—in 1897—in Scotland, and came to Newfoundland with her family when she was seven. Even though both of her parents have died and her sister has moved, she remains alone in the house in a place called Harry's Brook, despite the isolation, or maybe because of it. Her closest neighbour is eight miles away in the town of Gallants.

Harry's Brook isn't big enough to be a pinpoint on the Newfoundland map. The population is one: Miss Mary Cobb. There's no road in or out. The train serves as one of her only two links to the world. Her phone is the other and it connects her to the operator in Gallants and so to the rest of the world. Despite the isolation, Mary Cobb has a loving and caring community—it just moves on the rails.

Noon. Back to the house for lunch. Soup, milk, and a cookie. Wash up and out the door again, through the yard, through the gate, down to the field. Past houses that face the mountains or bay. Hamlet houses don't all face the same direction—they face whatever their owners want them to face. Mountains, a view of the sunset, sunrise, the bay.

For the first time in my life, I feel different. I'm eleven, but I feel older. Feel responsible. Trusted. But most of all, I feel old.

Walk around the hamlet. Meet someone on the road.

How are ye gettin' on, my dears?

Good. I answer for everyone.

Back to the house.

Supper. Help put the boys to bed. Almost end of the day.

My uncle smokes his cigar and reads the paper—billows of white smoke in the kitchen. My aunt reads a magazine.

Down to the bay and a walk on the shore. Music from somebody's radio. Tony Bennett—"Old Devil Moon." Perry Como. Elvis Presley. A Newfoundland folk song.

People are watering gardens, washing their cars, puttering with machinery, taking things in from the clothesline or putting things out. A man on a stepladder is trimming a rose trellis over his gate. His hair catches in thorns. He shakes his head free and waves hello.

How are ye gettin' on, my dear?

Good.

Well, it's got a few flaws, he says, referring to his job of trimming, *but a man on a galloping horse wouldn't notice it.* And he laughs. *Visiting your aunt and uncle, are ya?*

I tell him yes.

Quite the yarner, your uncle!

I tell him I know—that I heard the story about the man who saved his life with a nail.

Oh yes, my dear, we all heard that one.

When I'm walking along the shore, I'm walking on the absolute edge of North America. Traces of all types of seeds end up here as they're blowing towards the Atlantic. Seeds can't blow across the ocean to England, so they end up here, in Newfoundland—an assortment of flowers found nowhere else on the face of the earth.

That's probably why the Beothuk lived here—the space, and all the wildflowers. Smoke curling its way from their fire. Water nearby for fishing. All of them saying in their own Beothuk way, *How's yerself* and *God bless your cotton socks* and *It's a jacket colder than yesterday* and *Can't complain, b'y, can't complain.* Then a mug of hot tea before going into the wigwam. Everything calm and peaceful.

Nothing about my life is calm or peaceful—before school, in school, or after—except for the one week each year when no one is living on edge: the Atlantic Ocean and magnificent Bonne Bay. The cabin was deep in the woods and Bonne Bay is remote, but it's different. It's the ocean and bright painted dories. High crashing waves. It's our big canvas tent, which is generally waterproof. Thousands of blueberries. Smell of pine. Strong tea over a wide open fire. Hot soup beneath Newfoundland stars. Flaps over a tent window flying open at night, revealing pockets of sky and a moon. It's our only family vacation. It's the price of a tank of gas, but it's one full week inside the gates of heaven.

We travel to Bonne Bay in July or August and set up the tent in roughly the same spot every year—beneath the same trees, near the same rare, nameless flowers. The Coleman is at peace with itself, on the picnic table, not hanging from trees. My father fills every available space in the trunk—around the tent and the Coleman and the spare tire and the camping equipment—with samples of cookies. He's prepared for a sale at the edge of the ocean, for any store that happens to be at the edge of the world. I sell comic books from the car window. A crippled girl buys every *Little Lulu* I've ever owned in my life. I save them for her.

My mother taught me survival skills in Bonne Bay. *Make a loud sound and someone will hear you,* she said. *Or follow a river downstream. Someone always lives at the end of a river.*

Bonne Bay is the choir heard in the crashing of waves. Green and black seaweed tangled around driftwood and shells. A moon being swallowed by clouds. It's hundreds of birds, like colourful marbles. Smoke from a campfire touching the clouds. A Newfoundland sky filled with thousands of colours. Rose-coloured clouds wrapped across the horizon. It's train tracks and dandelion seeds floating like snow. People go to the water when they have a dilemma. It's as if the waves can wash troubles away.

I don't know why my mother feels safe during the night at Bonne Bay. It makes no sense, but she does. It's complete darkness except for the moon and the stars. The last breath of the fire stinging her eyes with its smoke—a sweet woodsy smell—a fire like the Beothuks'.

The light in the hamlet is starting to fade, and with it the warmth, and now it's cold. I'm not wearing a sweater. Leave the shore, back to the house, taste of a few berries along the way.

The setting sun flames like a jewel. Ruby light on silver water. Most of the sky is a flaming ball of pink fire. The rest is blue and silver. Just when you think it can't get any better, it does.

My uncle is standing on the porch. I point out the sunset—that it's beautiful.

You won't get any argument out of me, my luv.

I don't know why I feel different here, but I do. A good kind of different. As if I'm in a new country—could speak in a foreign language. My mind doesn't feel choked. That's not the right word. I don't have a word. I don't feel on edge or worried that I'll give the wrong answer, do the wrong thing, have someone chase me around the spare room with a butcher knife and then out to my uncle's car, or that a nun will tell me to fall to my knees and pray in the corner by the hooked rug. I'm not worried that my aunt will see a petrifying omen inside one of her teapots.

I stand at the open window, elbows on the ledge, face in my hands, soft, cool breeze through the room, wind moving branches, wind in my hair. Stars are scattered across the sky like pieces of diamond. *Enamel White* moon set in a *Dark Navy* sky.

If I look up, high in the sky, past the clouds and at that part of the sky that's directly behind the clouds—that changing blue space—that's where I'll walk, in my mind. Up to the clouds and beyond. Past all the stars and planets. Keeping my balance amid the fog and rain and snow. I'll walk across clouds and come to a rainbow and all the Hollywood stars who've passed on before me will be there together—James Dean, Rudolph Valentino, Jean Harlow, Carole Lombard, Hank Williams. And they'll be there with all the Beothuk, having tea under a rainbow. And I'll say, *How are ye gettin' on?* And they'll all say, *Best kind, my dear, best kind.*

That's a pilgrimage I can make every day of my life—up to the clouds. And they'll be so close I'll be able to touch them. And there'll be stars that no one has ever imagined—that no one could ever imagine existed. There'll be colours no paint chip ever came close to. Colours that don't even have names, they're that beautiful. And there'll be planets no one has heard of and I'll walk to the Milky Way and wander through some parts of the galaxy. And then I'll come to the moon, and I'll stop. Because it's so beautiful there's no reason to go any farther. I'll stay by the moon all night, with space all around me, and if people are out for a stroll past the Milky Way and the stars, I'll say, *How are ye gettin' on?* And they'll say, *Can't complain, my dear. How's yerself?*

And I'll say, *Best kind.*

The wildflowers in the jar are completely dead. I'll replace them tomorrow unless there's a miracle during the night. Pray, bed, sleep.

Chapter Five

WEDNESDAY *Day Five*

It's my fourth day waking up in the hamlet. Two Hail Marys and I'm out of bed.

Wide rays of sunlight are flooding the room. Whistle of morning birds. Smell of trees and fried eggs.

Each hamlet day begins, unfolds, and ends. Hail Mary, look out the window, make the bed. Wash, dress, down the stairs, into the kitchen. News and morning music. Breakfast. *Down the chute,* down to the field. Back up the road to the house. Lunch. Out the door, down to the field again, and around. Up to the house. I can smell supper all the way out to the gate. Boys to bed. Down to the shore, meet someone on the road.

How are ye gettin' on, my dear?

Good.

Back to the house, watch the eternally changing sky, the hamlet lights, and clouds being lit by a moon. Sleep. Dream.

Even though it's late June, it gets cold in the morning, so I pull the afghan around me and lean on the windowsill. The sun is white like a moon. Windows glisten like pieces of mirror, and the bay is like rolling silver. Wind ruffles the grass and the fields and blows through my hair.

People are starting out for the day. Doors open and close. Squeaking of hinges. A few cars pull from driveways. Seagulls glide like pieces of paper in a pink and blue and white-orange sky. Their wild sounds echo across the shoreline and above the people.

At home, my mother is gripping her first cup of tea for the day and reading her leaves with the penetrating look on her face. She lives in a world that's out of control and she wants control over everyone—especially me. But I'm already fully controlled by the nuns, have regular headaches and a tragic look on my face, and my head has been fully examined.

Last night, I dreamt in a foreign language—I have no idea what anything meant.

No matter where you go, you're going to be alone—go where you want to be alone. I heard that in a dream one time, so I go to Cobb Lane.

There are probably roads to heaven all over the world, but the one I can walk to, alone, is Cobb Lane—a ten-minute walk from our house but it could be a thousand miles away. Mountains, a pond with weeping willows sweeping the water, two gliding white swans, a sky as wide as the world, and a church steeple off in the distance. Beautiful homes are set back in gardens. If people are home, they're inside. High hedges and flowering trees close to the road. A wooden fence to hold onto. Whisper of wind. Rustle of trees, green against sky. A beautiful Tudor inn with hundreds of windows. Everything good converges there. Cobb Lane has nothing whatsoever to do with Miss Mary Cobb. It's by sheer coincidence.

Cobb Lane is a half-hour detour between the screaming nuns and my mother's cursing and yelling and the look on her face. For one half hour each day, there's stillness.

Wind swirls around me, the book bag pushes forward, and leaves do somersaults in an after-school breeze.

On Cobb Lane, I don't feel like a beggar. No one is raging. No leather straps.

When I look down at the swans and the pond, there's a space between me and the rest of the world and it's the space that I want. To see the world from a distance, not crowded on top of me.

If I need to cry, I can cry on Cobb Lane. I turn away from things that surround me, face only the swans, and let the tears fall. If someone walks by or a car passes through, they'll think, *How sweet—a little girl looking at swans.* On Cobb Lane, I'm a pigeon-toed missionary with an unreadable skull, walking a quiet path to enlightenment.

Nat King Cole is downstairs in the kitchen—"The Sand and the Sea." Sound of dishes, my aunt and uncle talking.

Wash, dress, down the stairs, through the hall, and into the kitchen. My uncle is leaving for work. *See you by and by.*

Morning news. Nikita Khrushchev. Marilyn Monroe married Arthur Miller but there's no mention of poor Joe DiMaggio. A report about offshore fishing. Time of the evening tide. Price of salt cod. Joey Smallwood. "The Ballad of Davy Crockett." A commercial for Rinso. The McGuire Sisters—"Sincerely."

My aunt brings my plate to the table—egg, hot buttered toast, and bacon. She brings the teapot, the regular one, and has her own breakfast. She puts laundry in the machine and I give her a few things of my own.

The two boys are up. Breakfast. *Down the chute.* Wash up, out the door, down the steps, out to the road, and down to the field. Gulls are making their screeching sounds and a black-and-white cat inches its way along a fence, crosses the sidewalk, crosses the road, and the two boys follow it with their eyes and shout. A plane overhead. A telephone ringing in somebody's house. Sounds of a hamlet morning—slow-moving traffic, a church bell, and children laughing.

The man with the trellis is correcting a flaw that he missed just in case a man on a galloping horse comes to a grinding halt and wants a closer inspection.

Matilda is weeding flowers next to her gate.

'Ow are ye gettin' on, my dear?

Good.

Not a word of a lie, now? she asks.

Not a word of a lie, I tell her, because it isn't.

The flowers in Matilda's yard begin on one side of the gate, cross the front of her yard, go along the side, around the back, up the other side, and around to the gate again. They circle the house and with it Matilda and her husband who can knit a bicycle if I give him a ball of steel wool.

My mother is probably on her way to the garden by now, at ten o'clock in the morning. She'll finish the housework, have a quick cup of tea and a fast read of her leaves, then outdoors to soften the earth around a wide bed of dahlias. Or trim the front hedge. Or make sure the wall of mile-a-minute is completely concealing the neighbours—or maybe it's herself she's concealing. The garden carries her through tragedy, poverty, despair, and self-imposed isolation. She lives in two worlds: inside the house with the demons and cursing, and outside in the world of her garden. And I live in the two worlds with her.

She plunges a shovel into the ground and the earth complies every year. I plant nasturtium seeds by the back door every spring, on either side of the steps. Plunge a tablespoon into the ground, cover the seeds with black dirt, and the result is exactly the same. Earth complies. Yellow and orange and rust-coloured blossoms, round green parasol leaves.

Matilda says her vegetables are planted at the back of her house, in the good soil—flowers don't need the best ground.

When this 'ouse was built, my dear, the people knew what they were doing. They didn't waste a drop of good earth.

She steps away from the weeding, rubs her hands on her apron, and examines the yard.

They built the 'ouse on top of the rocky part. You don't want to waste good soil by building your 'ouse right on top of it. Wilful waste makes woeful want. Look at the river before you take the ferry. And she winks.

I tell her *A stitch in time saves nine.* It's the only thing I can think of.

She waves to the boys, then goes back to her weeding, and I remember three sentences. No matter how long I live, I may never get them out of my mind.

End of spring, 1954. End of grade four. After pathological Saint Mary Genesius and for a few months we have Sister Mary Saint John the Baptist. If anything's broken, Sister Mary Saint John the Baptist is the one to repair it. She keeps a hammer inside her desk, and she doesn't use the tool as a weapon.

Three sentences in large flowing script are written on a side blackboard the day we enter her room, and they remain there for the rest of the year, in bright yellow chalk:

Small minds talk about people.

Average minds discuss events.

Great minds discuss ideas.

Monday through Friday, the three sentences stare at me. Dear God, don't let me have a small mind in addition to everything else—the bent head, the slightly pigeon-toed feet, the unreadable skull, the blank stares, and the tragic look on my face. But all I can do is wonder why people who discuss events are superior to those who talk about people. How can you discuss an event without discussing the people who are in the event? I may never get the three sentences out of my mind.

Every day, I look at the sayings on the board. Learn arithmetic and spelling. Walk to the front of the room for a strap. Fall to my knees, recite something written in Latin. Up off my knees. Reading and conjugation. Prayer at the end of the day. Leave the room in an orderly fashion.

We're praying a minimum of five times a day. Any occasion, any excuse. We pray during the Hungarian Revolution. When Queen Elizabeth goes to Australia. When one of the Dionne quintuplets dies. To save our imperfect souls from the hot flames of hell.

One day I'm listening to *The Lone Ranger* on the radio—*A fiery horse with the speed of light, a cloud of dust, and a hearty 'Hi-Yo, Silver!'*—and the next day I'm knocked on the head with a pointer or kneel in a corner with my right index finger pressed to my lips. I'm living in sin with a Presbyterian.

Down the road, past gardens and houses and fences and fields and the racket of gulls. People are weeding and hoeing and yelling from one yard to another.

Yer vegetables doing well, b'y?

Weed in summer, eat in winter, b'y.

I'll go bail for that, b'y.

You'll never plough a field by turning it over in yer mind.

I mumble *A stitch in time saves nine* under my breath.

Sounds of a hamlet morning, sounds of the bay. The fields are a green and gold landscape. The roads are spools of unravelling silver ribbon. Everywhere there are people with hands in the soil.

The first ones with hands in the soil were the Beothuk and they didn't need ploughs. They knew where to find the best berries and roots and they built wigwams right on the spot. Then the Vikings, who were hopeless at coping with Newfoundland's weather, tried to grow crops but left after two years and took their boats back to Greenland and Norway. Then Christopher Columbus and John Cabot and fleets of invaders. They came only for fish so there was no point in planting. Then explorers and settlers learned to adapt to rocky terrain and unbearable winters, killed all the Beothuk, and learned what could grow in Newfoundland soil.

And while everyone had their hands in the soil, the bay never changed. Two hundred years before Matilda moved from the outport, the bay and sky and wind were exactly the same. Everyone next to their house or their wigwam, touching the earth.

A black horse wanders its way through a neighbouring field. *Black Beauty* comes to life right before me. Wide open blue sky, a wooden fence, and a very calm, wandering horse, nose to the ground and the smell of sweet grass.

Look at the horse! It's eating a lot of grass for its dinner.

Why?

Because ... it didn't have breakfast.

Why?

Quick! Look at the schooner!

A three-masted schooner sits in the bay like a scene from *Captains Courageous. Black Beauty* and *Captains Courageous* right here in the hamlet. Its white sails are triangles on a geometry template and they lean against a *Cornflower Blue* sky. Gulls circle the boat and perch on the rigging.

If this were the actual *Captains Courageous*, it would be seconds before the screen says *The End* and the young boy on board is no longer a brat. He's calmed down after spending three months at sea with the kind fisherman who saved his life from the ocean. He learned to fish and take care of the ship as the crew sailed along the Newfoundland coast. It would be after the terrible accident when the kind fisherman drowns. It would be the end of the movie. The schooner would be in port, the boy and his father would reunite and throw wreaths in the bay in memory of all the drowned fishermen, and there wouldn't be a dry eye inside the Majestic Theatre.

Pop, my father's father, had his own schooner, named *The Kimberly*. He brought food and clothes to isolated people living in coves along the Newfoundland coast. In 1907, four years before my father was born, Pop sailed to Labrador with a captain, a crew, and a full cargo. But they were overcome in a terrible storm and had to jump for their lives, and what happened next involved Pop, a lumber camp, and Sir Wilfred Grenfell—a physician and the founder of the Grenfell Mission. Grenfell devoted his life to what Jesus would have done if he'd been a medical doctor. My father probably thought the same exact thing as he drove on the treacherous roads: *What would Jesus have done if he'd been a confectionery salesman and a salesman of house paint?*

The lumber camp had a tug named *Ethel Jean* and the men didn't like Pop because he was Lebanese. They saw the damaged *Kimberly* the day after the storm, and before Pop could return to the schooner, they stole his entire cargo of dry goods.

The same week, Grenfell arrived in his hospital steamer and Pop told him about the terrible storm—that his crew had to jump for their lives—and that the lumber company stole his entire cargo before he could return to the schooner. The lumber company's captain swore that he took everything because *The Kimberly* was completely abandoned. Pop's captain swore the cargo was Pop's. Pop swore the cargo was his and said he wanted it back. Grenfell agreed to be Justice of the Peace, and settled the case.

Several documents survive to this day, but the final statement is completely destroyed. Only a fragment remains, showing the very last line: *I hand over all my property to do with as you think best.* And it's signed with Pop's *X*.

No one knows if Pop received compensation in exchange for his goods or if the lumber company stole everything.

A few years later, Pop built the store in the hamlet, and here I am taking care of the two boys while my uncle takes care of the store.

Pop succumbed to his broken hip and my mother bowed her head at his funeral. It was the only time in my life that I saw her say anything close to a prayer.

In his autobiography, Grenfell mentions treacherous Newfoundland fog, visits to Asia Minor, his conversations with Alexander Graham Bell, and building Newfoundland hospitals. But there's no mention of Pop's cargo of dry goods. The only thing missing in Grenfell's autobiography is what happened to Pop.

Pop was buried and there was no mention of Grenfell at his funeral.

Pop was the only authentic corpse I ever saw in my life except for skeletons in movies. A polished brown, satin-lined coffin, a rosary in his pale cold hands, his broken hip hidden from view. And I kissed him goodbye as he lay dead and cold. A footstool up to the casket. We all kissed him goodbye.

Pop worked hard every day of his life, against almost insurmountable odds, and my mother, who understands insurmountable odds, bowed her head. And there were bouquets of flowers. And Lebanese food. A table decorated with beautiful cards. There were people and vases of flowers everywhere. He'd never had so much company.

The schooner pulls away from the bay, the horse moves to a new section of field, and it's almost noon.

At noon, my father is parking his Chevrolet close to the gate. My mother makes lunch, pours two cups of tea, then reads her own leaves. They both finish lunch. My father makes the sign of the cross, pushes his chair away from the table, and out to the road. He ends every meal with a prayer.

Everyone in my life prays, except for my mother. I wish she did. It might help with the demons. An empty chapel, away from noises inside the house, haunting sound of the pipes, the house settling in for the night, branches scraping a window, shadows on walls. A quiet chapel moment with light spilling through stained glass windows. A room where a person can think. Even Mr. Clark would say a prayer in thanksgiving. For the eggs—the perfect ones, in particular.

Even Miss Mary Cobb may utter a word of thanks for her view—sweet smell of earth, mist on the mountains. Thanksgiving for a warm shawl and a mug of hot tea. For the largest fort on the face of the earth. But she's the only inhabitant of Harry's Brook, so her desire to pray would have to be personal. There's no one to warn her of total damnation in hell if she doesn't. Plus, there's the additional factor. Mary Cobb is Presbyterian.

Up the road. Pass Matilda along the way. She's talking to someone on the porch, sees me, and waves a big hello.

'Ow's everything going, my dear?

Good, I yell back, because everything is.

I should find it easy to talk in the hamlet, to have long conversations, but I don't. Mr. Clark is the only one I'm able to talk to and I don't know why it should be that way, but it is. No one is yelling or strapping me here, or pounding answers into my mind or telling me I shouldn't be so stupid. But whenever I speak, my own voice sounds like an echo or a recording. And it's playing at the same exact time that I'm speaking, and the echo distracts me. I get confused by the sound of my own voice and the voice of the echo and I have no idea how many voices are talking. So I try not to speak. I don't know how people on the radio do it. No idea how Margot Davies does it week after week.

Up the road, past houses that face the mountains or bay, through the gate, up the front steps, and there's a smell of cooking all the way out to the door. Sounds from the radio. News of the world. A report from the fisheries. Hank Williams. "Squid Jiggin' Ground."

It's the first rainy evening.

Fog covers the bay like a veil. Not even a breeze. Only stillness, oncoming rain, and flashes of silent lightning.

When we lived in the woods, the cabin had a long, narrow sun porch. It ran the entire front of the house and was the only room with real light. Windows looked into the faces of trees and a strawberry field at the top of a hill. If there was a storm during strawberry season and we had enough warning, we'd sit behind the glass windows, watching lightning explode, eating berries with sugar and milk. It felt extremely luxurious. Like a photograph in a Hollywood magazine—*Photoplay* or *Movieland.* Inside the cabin and safe, watching fireworks light up the sky, eating wild strawberries with sugar and milk, the air thick with rain. Then long rays of light would pour from the sky, like a scene from the Bible. Light spilled from heaven, straight down to the roof and through it—straight down to me in a chair, eating berries.

After every storm, nature reassembles itself—the flowers and creatures and trees. Nature reassembles itself even after a forest fire. The most noticeable thing about burnt forest is silence. Creatures have run for their lives or gone underground. Thousands of acres have gone up in flames. Tall grey trees that will never come back. Then the ground covers itself with the spikes of red fireweed plants. Nature carpets the ground with a reflection of fire.

Well by the hole in my coat, Mr. Clark would probably say.

Flowers and weeds return first, then small trees, insects, and birds. But it takes years to put it all back together again. It takes decades to retell a forest.

Well by the hole in my coat. Now that's a story.

Margaret! We're putting the kettle on. Would you like a cup of tea and a piece of toast? my aunt calls up from downstairs.

I grab my sweater, run down the stairs, through the hall, past the window with white lace curtains and pots of red geraniums, past Saint Francis of Assisi on one wall and a portrait of the two boys on the other, past the living room, and into the kitchen. My uncle is sitting at the table finishing his evening cigar, my aunt is pouring tea, bread is popping out of the toaster, and the room smells of hot buttered toast. It's nine o'clock and the rain is coming down hard.

Did you hear about the storm last night in Nova Scotia? my uncle asks us.

No, I tell him. I didn't hear anything.

My aunt hasn't heard about it either. *What happened?* she asks as she puts a plate of toast and a pot of hot tea on the table. The teapot is red. *Fire Engine Red.* It could be in the spare room with everything else.

A guy came into the store and told me all about it. He said it was all the news in Nova Scotia today. All over the radio.

My aunt and I both missed hearing about it.

Heavy winds—brutal heavy winds. We may be getting the start of it now.

I didn't hear that, my aunt says. She pours tea for each of us. We're on our own with the toast.

Sudden cold temperature and heavy fog, too—thick as pea soup. I'm surprised you didn't hear about it this afternoon. Nobody mentioned it?

I never heard a word, my aunt says.

My uncle reaches for a slice of toast and applies a thick layer of strawberry jam. He pours milk and sugar into his cup and stirs his tea.

Yes, my dear. Heavy winds and freezing-cold temperature. The guy said it was so cold every woodhorse in Nova Scotia was trying to get into a barn. It was all on the news. Hundreds of galloping woodhorses spotted all over Nova Scotia. And he takes a long sip of his tea.

Not a word of a lie. Thousands of galloping woodhorses in Nova Scotia. You'll see it in the paper tomorrow.

My aunt rolls her eyes and mutters something under her breath and once again I can't hear what she's saying.

When it gets dark in the hamlet, it gets cold, as well. And now there's cold from the rain. I go upstairs, put on my pyjamas, move the three pillows for the fiftieth time, and stand at the closed window. Except for rain dripping from trees, it's quiet. Only layers of grey in the sky.

At night, I can see the same exact things that I saw during the day. Trees, the gardens, the clothesline, mountains, houses, roads. Nothing changes, except light—or the lack of it. I think it's the lack that my mother fears. She doesn't feel safe until she has the blanket over her head, windows sealed tight, furniture moved against doors. She covers her head with a blanket so whatever is in the dark closet can't come out to get her at night. Some people say she's the nervous type but I think something or someone drove her insane. I know, because I'm under the blanket with her. And in four days, I'll be back in her bed.

Lights in the houses are fading. Large patches of darkness. In the hamlet, when people turn out their lights, the hamlet is turned out as well.

I hear a cupboard door open and close. Someone stirring their tea. Someone is opening and closing the screen door. I can hear its creaking sound. My aunt is setting the table for breakfast. Clink of dishes and moving of chairs. I can smell the smoke from my uncle's cigar, hear sounds of the night. Swirling wind. Feel of cold air on my body. Dripping rain from the roof. Hum of the night. Whisper of trees. Light from the moon on the floorboards as the sky begins to clear. Moonlight on whitewashed fences. Blue light on a bay in the distance. That's what I'm seeing and hearing. Seeing a new part of the world through a spare-room window.

This is how the Beothuk listened at night. The lapping of waves. Scent of coyote. Cry of the wolves. Their own children stirring. Rushing of wind. Sound of the rain. Wild animals sneaking their way through the camp. Sweet smell from a crackling fire. An animal rooting through leaves. Sounds from beneath the earth. Sounds of their own hearts beating. Voice of wind singing through forest. Songs of their ancestors.

Chapter Six

THURSDAY *Day Six*

It's six o'clock in the morning. No one else in the house is awake and the sun has given up on trying to break through grey and white clouds. It's misty, mauzy, and grey and I'll probably stay inside all day with the boys.

I dreamt of weather last night. Rain was falling like claps of thunder and ripped branches from trees. It severed thousands of leaves and sent all of them flying. If you looked up, you could see sheets of thundering silver rain, and people were running for cover with children and pets and belongings. It was as if Niagara had been completely uprooted and was now in the sky and was thundering down on an entire population. No one cared if you panicked. No one cared if you were screaming at the top of your lungs. Everyone was. And the rain drowned out everyone's sound. There was nothing to do except save your own life and someone else's if you could do that—no one was making judgments. There was only rain like Niagara turned upside down. I hid on a porch, in the corner, as walls around parks crumbled and fell to the ground in pieces. Someone drowned in the downpour. Slabs of concrete fell in front of running, screaming people. I don't remember how long I stayed on the porch. I don't remember where I went. I know I left my hiding place, but I woke up. I don't know where the birds went. I wasn't thinking about them, but I fear the worst.

My dreams are getting so complicated that they don't seem believable, even to me. I never dream about school. Never dream about nuns. But I remember them every day of my life and what I remember the most is what doesn't happen. It's mid-morning, before recess. It's late afternoon, just before we're released for the day. *Released* is a word that works well when I think about nuns—we are released. It's just after lunch. It's before the day begins. It's raining or snowing or sunny. It's Christmas or Easter. It's early June, just before we take our final exam. Pass or fail. Heaven or hell. There's no mention of a possible time spent in purgatory and being touched by the hot flames, then allowed to move on. It's heaven or hell. What I remember the most is what doesn't happen. There's silence. No one speaks. No one sighs. No one moves in their seat, turns their head, looks to the side, shifts their feet, or—God Almighty, Jesus, and Mary forbid—whispers. This is what I remember the most. Every day of my life with the nuns—what doesn't happen.

We enter the room in the morning in an orderly fashion, go to our desks, sit on our seats, and wait for the bell to ring. The nun hits the top of a small silver bell and we stand, pray, sit down again. The day begins. Something is written in chalk on the board. I try to remember. Words are spoken—nun words—and I try to remember them all. Recess—fifteen minutes. Back inside. Stand. Pray. Sit. Look at the board. Listen. Try to remember. Put one book away, take out another. Look at the board. Listen. Try to remember it all. Out at the end of the day. Talk to someone I know. Walk to Cobb Lane. Home and my mother's affliction. Pray, eat, pray. Homework. Look out the window. Pray. Sleep. Dream. Up again, repeat. No one moves. No one speaks. What I remember the most is what doesn't happen.

Wash, dress, make the bed, move the pillows—all without making a sound. Pray. Creep down the stairs and into the kitchen. I can feel and smell rain in the air. It's a good time to take a walk by myself before a possible downpour. Look for a different road in a new part of the hamlet.

I put the kettle on for a cup of hot tea. A mug of Red Rose for the walk. Everything echoes. The floorboards creak, the kettle screams. The cupboard door hinges. The spoon in the cup.

Taking a mug of hot tea to a new part of the hamlet feels very adventurous. Like Katharine Hepburn—courageous and mighty. I'm in charge of two children's lives for a week and heading into the wilds like Katharine in *The African Queen.* I'll be wandering through mist in a long yellow slicker, with a mug of hot tea.

I feel a sense of belonging here. The spare room, the window, the shore when I'm walking alone. No damaging words. It won't last forever—in September, I'll be beaten back into submission—but for the moment, I'm Katharine Hepburn.

Up the road, past the church, which is closed for the week unless there's a funeral or a wedding. Around the corner and down a different road. As far as the eye can see, I'm the only thing moving. The hamlet is silent—only the crackle of raindrops on leaves. Branches are heavy with rain. Smell of wet soil, trees, wildflowers, and moss, and dew covers it all without breaking a blade of grass. It's a miracle. *By the hole in my coat,* Mr. Clark would probably say, *I think you're right. It's a miracle!*

The trees in this part of the hamlet are silver birch. The Beothuk used the bark for building canoes and wigwams. There's a remarkable difference between a forest of birch and a forest of spruce. Spruce trees spread themselves out—their boughs droop like wide heavy curtains, and everything in front and behind is concealed. But the lower half of a birch tree is bare. You can easily see what's in front and what you've just passed.

Birds are whistling and anticipating the sun. There's never a bird off by itself, sulking, without a branch of its own. Somehow they all find room. A grey rabbit rushes through damp weeds and grass. It stops, stares at me with big, black, glassy eyes filled with terror, then runs for its life. I'm not a threat, but tell that to the rabbit. I've probably eaten part of its family.

I'm nine years old. It's the middle of winter and cold as a tomb. It's just after we moved into town.

Two hunters show up at the front door with long, dangling, dead rabbits. The men wear high heavy boots and thick jackets to withstand frigid Newfoundland winds, when cold eats its way to the bone and stays there. They offer the rabbits for sale, are invited into the house, and leave a trail of wet snow on the clear plastic runner from the front door straight to the kitchen. The rabbits are stretched out, stomach-side up, and inspected on top of the table. They look like giant lucky charms—except they're bad luck now if ever there was any. The rabbits are purchased and skinned, and broken so they can fit inside pans. Their flesh is sewn together, then cooked. It was sometimes the only food that we had and we had to be grateful, but I hated every bite that ever slid down my throat. They tasted like forest—like flowers and leaves. Like loss of freedom.

Something grey, the colour of rock—something clumsy and loud—moves beneath branches. A wild turkey, frightened by footsteps, quickly and stately swaggers away.

There's a fast-moving brook a few feet off the shoulder, and I follow it on ground that the Beothuk probably walked on before me.

A cream-coloured mushroom has attached itself to the base of a birch. My father's paint chips would call it *Off-White, Light Ivory*, or *Buff.* The mushroom is fragile and wide like a fan—like something Scarlett O'Hara would fan herself with on a hot day in Tara.

As I'm thinking about Scarlett O'Hara, something brown gallops across the brook, then freezes in front of me, ten feet away. I stop dead. It stops dead. Three other fast-moving brown things stop dead and I stare into the eyes of four deer, in the drizzle, beneath birch trees laden with rain. God help me! I don't have a gun—only my half-empty mug—but they're on guard. I may as well be armed.

The mother is motionless. Fierce brown eyes and smell of trap in her nostrils. The fawns move around her. They're fragile, and are restless like children. They're not yet familiar with fear.

I bow my head slowly in a sign of goodwill. I don't know what else to do. My neck is so stiff with fright that I can barely get it to move. I don't want to drop the mug—she might think it's a threat. I don't know what she's thinking. I barely know what I'm thinking myself.

I turn around—slowly, slowly, slowly—and head back towards the road and the house. I can feel their eyes on the back of my neck. The ground is slippery and my footsteps are silent. I take a few very slow steps—a false casual slowness. I pretend to know what I'm doing. I look back, almost without turning my head. My eyes turn around but my head doesn't move. Nothing has changed. They're watching my every move. It's four wild deer against me, and I'm in their woods. If there's a showdown, I have only a mug.

I walk to the road, and my heart is pounding so hard I can see it. I look back and they've vanished. There's only me, in a wet yellow slicker, and a useless, clumsy grey turkey somewhere off in the distance.

My shoes and socks are completely soaked and the fog is lingering.

In the house, my uncle is sitting down for his breakfast and calls out as I walk through the door: *Come in out of the wet!*

I saw deer.

Go away with ya!

I did—four of them.

My aunt pulls a chair from the table. *Sit down and have breakfast. You'll be dry as a bone in no time.*

I put on a pair of dry socks and sit at the kitchen table with my uncle and aunt, and we have our tea and hot toast and eggs, and the radio plays "The Wayward Wind," and I wonder if the things that go through their minds are anything at all like the things that go through my own.

I'm ten years old. Late spring. 1955. *The Bob Cummings Show* and *The Millionaire.* The United States is performing nuclear tests in Nevada. Danny Thomas, Elvis Presley, and Loretta Young. Grace Kelly and Marlon Brando win an Academy Award, Winston Churchill resigns, and Canada wins the Ice Pairs Championship at Vienna. "The Ballad of Davy Crockett." The Warsaw Pact. Rocky Marciano and Nikita Khrushchev. *The Red Buttons Show.* March of Dimes leaflets on the kitchen table. Women in afternoon dresses at the dining-room table. Tea leaves on every table. Reading of cups. Don't spill salt on the table—it's bad luck. Don't put your keys on the table—bad luck. Don't cross knives on the table—bad luck. Never thirteen at the table—really bad luck. Don't ever put shoes on a table—bad luck. Keys and tables and salt. Tea leaves and knives and bad luck. It's probably wise to just avoid tables.

It's after a school day and women in patterned afternoon dresses are sitting at the dining-room table for tea and a reading of leaves. Everything's finished well before any husband comes home from work. Every man's supper has been planned well in advance—something's already cooked and just has to be heated up in the oven. Every woman is a non-Catholic, although I don't know if that's a requirement. One woman is so thin *you can see the sins on her soul*—that's what my mother says.

The women once went bowling and skating and fishing, just like my mother, and took courses in typing and shorthand so they could move up in the world. They wore fur hats above beautiful suits in the fall and drew a line on the back of their legs with a pencil during the Second World War—stockings were scarce and expensive and the line gave the look of a seam. They mailed letters to loved ones who'd been shipped overseas. But that was the past. Now, they want to see into their future with the help of my mother and a cluster of leaves in bone china cups edged with roses and gold. Will the women have happiness, illness, good fortune, or, God forbid, death?

My mother's skin is smooth and clear, probably due to the egg-white concoctions. And with her *Fire Engine Red* lipstick, her thick, wavy dark hair, rosy Maybelline cheeks, soft pastel cardigan, and small white pearl earrings, she looks especially pretty—the prettiest one at the table. But she's not fully present. She stares into the distance. *Far as ever a puffin flew.* Life up the highway has taken a toll. An emptiness, a blank look, envelops her face as the women chat about their families. Her mind is elsewhere. God knows where.

The cloth-covered table is set with Wedgwood plates, date squares, and small, crustless sandwiches. Pastry shells filled with canned lobster or crab. Homemade fudge in three flavours. A bouquet of flowers from somebody's garden. Glasses of dandelion wine—home brew from our basement. The dining-room curtains are closed.

I'm home in time to see the women finish their lunch and prepare for a reading. I pretend I'm invisible. In an hour, I'll devour a sandwich, a date square, and a filled pastry shell if there are any left over. The sofa's just a few feet away from the dining room, so I land there and listen and read and observe and think about food, and as long as I'm silent, which is an easy state for me to be in, no one will notice me.

My mother reaches for the bone china teapot, refills each woman's cup, and moves the food to a sideboard. I keep one eye on the food and one eye on the women, and pretend to be reading. Each tilt of the cup, each final sip of the tea, will predict illness, love, money, or mail. Each woman turns her cup upside down in its saucer. Leaves shift inside and her fate is sealed right there in our dining room. It's now good news or doom. Their lives are in the hands of my mother. She's simply the vessel through which words and images flow.

When my mother is scared, which is most of the time, she looks straight ahead—a dead stare, as if she's watching a movie the rest of us can't begin to imagine. As I watch her prepare, I know she's seeing the invisible images. I watch to see who'll become wealthy and who'll fall in love—although they're all married, so that never seems like a probable outcome. By my calculation, they can have illness, money, or mail. My mother slowly revolves each woman's cup, observing the leaves, and then—with a sombre, penetrating look on her face—she reveals each woman's future. She holds their ominous and inescapable future right there in the palm of her hand.

Every day, my mother reads leaves and my father prays. Not simultaneously. On separate occasions. My father goes in a minimum of four directions at once—addressing the present, praying the rosary, keeping an eye on my mother's affliction, and being strict with me. He's not extreme like the nuns, but he wants order. And if I can figure out what the order is that he wants and keep it, there isn't much trouble. That's what I've been trying to do for the past six years with the nuns, but I have more success with my father.

My uncle finishes breakfast, takes a last sip of his tea, makes the sign of the cross, pushes his chair from the kitchen table, and puts on his raincoat just in case there's a downpour.

See you by and by.

The boys are awake. I put eggs on to boil, slide one slice of bread into the toaster, pour a cup of hot tea for myself, and the day unfolds inside the house, safe from the drizzle and rain. Colouring books, trucks, and stories. The boys drag crayons across the page with the goal of making cowboys and fire trucks disappear from the paper. They make no attempt to stay within any lines—in fact, they defy them.

In grade three, I was informed that I coloured too deep. The nun said I coloured too thick. I was ordered to colour like everyone else. Pastel. The act of pressing a crayon into the paper was probably releasing the anxiety of the first eight years of my life. The paper was newsprint—scrap rolls from the town paper mill. Newsprint is thin and easy to rip, especially for me, since I'd apparently been colouring too thick all my life. But if I said anything remotely like *My paper is ripped*, she'd say, *Good carpenters don't complain about their tools*, and touch her rosary and give me the evil eye. So I'd piece the picture together with spit and draw a dark bird soaring through a dried-spit newspaper sky, and if I ripped the paper again, my supply of spit was endless.

In grade five, a teacher came to Newfoundland from the mainland. She wasn't a nun. She was worldly and taught art in the school auditorium for one hour each week, and she let me colour with deep, thick strokes, and I could use whatever crayons I wanted. She even asked me my favourite colour. It was the first time anyone had asked. It was purple. Very dark purple.

Finally, permission to be at peace with the wax.

She spoke about drawing in ways I had never imagined. *When you draw mountains, think of how old they are. When you're drawing a flower, think about roots. Every flower has roots.*

Kindergarten was *David* and *Ann* and knowing the difference. Sister Bernadette was grade one and there was no one like her ever again. Grade two was the furnace room and grade three was our first year of life in the woods. Grade four was another year in the woods and the evil Mary Genesius—a nun filled with so much venom and hate it's hard to believe she was ever a person. Grade five was permission to be at peace with the crayons. To have the thoughts I have in my mind. To think about things in my own way.

❖

It's eight o'clock. My uncle is in the living room, reading the paper. A thin white cloud of cigar smoke. The hamlet is settling in for the night. The grey morning sky has given way to dark patches of blue and a few scattered stars—a sky in the process of clearing itself.

I stand on the porch for a while, then go inside and look at a magazine. It's their house and I'm a visitor, even though I'm a relative and have been babysitting the two boys for almost a week. I feel awkward after the boys are in bed. I'm not sure where I belong. And I don't want to just barge into the living room and spread myself out on a chair.

Their magazines are next to the phone. *Popular Mechanics. Maclean's. The Hockey News.* Magazines about furniture. Newfoundland stories. My parents consider magazines a complete waste of good money. We have free Sears catalogues that arrive four times a year, pamphlets from African missions, and *The Reader's Digest. The Farmers' Almanac* isn't really a magazine—it's more like an instructional booklet. My mother lives by *The Farmers' Almanac.* Weather, predictions, the horoscope. Phases of the moon. Folk medicine cures. To extract the core of a boil, fill a jar with hot water, empty the jar, wait a few seconds, then place the hot mouth right on top of the skin over the boil. As the jar cools, the core will come out. This has to be perfect, because if the jar is blistering hot, the patient—in this case, me—can be severely burned.

And we have the radio guide. On Saturday evenings, after supper and after a semblance of calm has settled over our house, while everyone else is asleep or preparing for sleep, I sit in the kitchen, feet on a chrome chair, listening to whatever CBC offers. Sometimes the only sounds in the house are the hum of the fridge, me shifting my feet on a chair, and a very low radio voice. BBC. *Late Night Theatre.* A waltz. Then the queen and sign-off.

It's difficult to know exactly what we want out of life, but it's relatively simple to know what we don't. We don't want abuse and chaos. We don't want to be perpetually living in fear. We want someone we can honestly trust—someone who will do us no harm. So Perry Como, Rosemary Clooney, Pat Boone, and Patsy Cline become that. And anything to do with the French language. I can't understand a word except *bonjour, au revoir,* and *merci beaucoup,* but I love the sound of the voices and if they're complaining or fighting I'm immune. It's like a foreign vacation right there in the kitchen.

I accept whatever the radio offers and go where it takes me. News of the world and weather reports. The *Hit Parade* countdown. Classical music. A report on the financial troubles of some religious organization—send money and they'll pray for me. I do enough praying on my own—I don't need them. A weekly connection to an outside world. Safety inside a radio. The radio offers escape from the nuns, from my mother's rage and affliction, from everything around me. Then upstairs and recitation of night prayers. I pray at night for the same reason I pray at all other times: if I don't, I'll be banished to hell or trapped forever in purgatory, which is just one step away from living in limbo.

I make a space on the kitchen table large enough for my elbows and put my chin in my hands. The boys are asleep. The kitchen is quiet. I miss the sounds from a radio.

The three massive pillows are moved once again, but I'm not ready for sleep. Something has happened this week and I'm not even sure what it is or how to explain it to myself or anyone else. Too many thoughts are rushing around in my mind.

Downstairs, my aunt is setting the table again for the morning. The cupboard doors open and close. The spicy smell of cigar will fill the house until well after my uncle is done for the evening.

My mother and father both smoke, although my mother smokes more than my father. Everyone smokes except for the nuns. Even the priests are smoking. Most of the movie stars smoke. Magazines are filled with pictures of smoking celebrities.

Margaret, we're having a cup of tea.

It's like music. She would never believe it or understand it, but it's almost like music. And I can't even explain that to myself.

When you're waiting for something to change, that's all you can think about, and most of the time we don't even know what it is that we want. We just know we want things to change for the better.

We have our tea and toast and strawberry jam and my uncle speaks.

Now, did you ever hear a story like this one? My aunt and I apply more jam to our toast and listen.

An Irish priest down in St. Mary's, a Father Duffy, wanted to build a church. This was 1835, and St. Mary's was just a handful of families, but Duffy wanted that church. The magistrate, a non-Catholic from England, wouldn't give him permission, but Father Duffy built the church anyway. Well, now the magistrate was beside himself and built a fish flake right in front of the church door. Then Father Duffy got beside himself and told his parishioners to burn the flake down, and eight of them did. Now, this was 13 January 1835.

Father Duffy got arrested, but when the police came back for the eight parishioners, the men chased the police and said they'd knock them to kingdom come if they ever came back.

My uncle takes a long sip of his tea.

Well, the British governor sent for a warship. Can you imagine? A warship against eight old Newfoundland churchgoers down in St. Mary's.

Now, Father Duffy had studied law, so he got himself released and persuaded the eight men to surrender, and said he'd defend them in court. So they all started their day-and-a-half trek to St. John's.

Well, the men got tired and wanted a cup of tea, but they couldn't find water. Father Duffy walked to a rock, gave it a mighty whack with his walking stick, and out gushed water. The men were sure they were seeing a miracle. They filled their kettle and made a cup of hot tea, had supper, and went to sleep for the night. When they got to St. John's, Father Duffy won the case and the men were released.

The men told the story to the people back home—about water gushing out from a rock. People believed it had to be some kind of miracle and went to the rock and prayed. Now, that was over a hundred years ago, and water is still gushing to this very day. And people still go there to pray. People from all over the world go there for miraculous water. They call it "Father Duffy's Well." And that's the God's honest truth.

And for the very first time, my aunt doesn't mumble. *I heard something about that,* she says. But she wants to see it herself.

My uncle swears it's *not a word of a lie*—which means it could be a whopper. *Yes, my dear, miraculous water like Lourdes,* and he'll take us all there someday. My aunt wants to see it before she'll believe it.

Not a word of a lie, my dear. Newfoundland has miraculous water, and he puffs on the cigar and leans back in his chair as if he owns part of that rock.

Something about these days in the hamlet has changed me a little. Being in charge of somebody's life, walking alone in the woods, the gravel shoreline, being trusted to do the right thing without somebody waiting in ambush.

I hope my mother's fear of the night and fear of the dark and fear of the unknown go away. That she'll stop seeing the demons—stop cursing and slamming things. That she'll stop seeing graveyards and ghosts in the dark. Stop seeing creeping things waiting outside the window. That she'll be done once and for all with the affliction. That she'll have peace in her mind and won't have the urge to chase me right through the house with a knife.

I'll have to endure my blank stares, nosebleeds, and slightly pigeon-toed feet. The tragic look on my face—that's inevitable. I'll have to endure the nuns—their violence and hatred and insults—but it won't last forever. Unless they manage to kill me completely.

A white moon is floating in a sea of *Dark Navy Blue.* I wish on the stars and I make a wish on the moon—the same moon that's lighting the forest for a deer and her three restless children.

The hamlet is beginning to turn out its lights. A hamlet that's offered itself to me for almost a week, and I didn't even know that I needed it, or that it was here.

Chapter Seven

FRIDAY *Day Seven*

Last night I dreamt about commas. I was at the depths of an ocean and I had large books in my hand and I was trying to swim through seaweed and fish and not drop the books, and as I got close to the top of the water, commas and eyes began to appear. They were everywhere. I tried not to look, and to concentrate on swimming and books and seaweed and fish and keeping it all together and getting to the top of the water. But it was probably all too much for me, because I woke up before I ever reached land.

The sunlight is bursting its way through the spare-room window and I have to squint. It's like the glare from a light bulb—like Mr. Clark's light for inspecting eggs, which have to be perfect.

When you look out the spare-room window, the first thing you notice in the morning is sunlight and what it does to the hamlet. Because so many of the fences and barns are whitewashed, the light is especially brilliant. A *Glossy White* paint chip.

The sun warms my face as I lean on the window ledge and the wind blows my hair away from my face.

Some people are working in gardens already and I can hear shovels plunging into the ground—can hear voices outside on the road.

How are ye gettin' on?

Best kind, b'y. How's yerself?

Can't complain, b'y! Can't complain. Then sound of a shovel again.

A crow hovers nearby, watching what's being unearthed. Others are huddled in trees like bandits. There are so many I don't bother to count. The crows take what the gulls don't want—or maybe it's the other way around.

The bay, with the blazing white sun, looks like a sea of white ice. Thin lines of white clouds are low in the sky, like roads—long Newfoundland roads in the winter.

I'm nine years old. It's the middle of winter. Early evening. Ice on the ground. Ice in the air. Roads are treacherous.

My father leans on the radiator in an upstairs bedroom and looks at the icy street below. He almost just killed a boy, he says. The boy cut across the road on a sleigh in front of the car and slid between the wheels.

It was a miracle I didn't kill him, he says.

Tears flood his eyes. Tears in his voice. A strange, terrified look on his face.

Blue twilight engulfs him. I don't know how. He's my father and he's standing in front of me crying and I don't know how to hold him. But the blue winter light does. It holds him as he looks through the window, down to the road, tears on his face.

Margaret, I almost just killed a boy. He says it as if he's in a confessional.

One of the things I learned from my father is to always keep moving. Unlike people who pray for things to come true in the future, my father prays that frightening things from the past will never happen again. That he won't almost kill a boy on the icy roads. The boy who went under his car on a sled. Miraculously unharmed. My father prays that will never happen again. He prays that Newfoundland will never have another depression. He was a teenager during the hungry years—that's what it was called in Newfoundland. He prays that he won't lose his job as a travelling salesman, after losing his store and its entire inventory and then losing our home. He prays to God Almighty and Jesus—don't ever let that happen again.

He prays that he'll always be able to take care of my mother and her affliction. So he kneels by the side of their bed, head bowed in silence, black rosary beads tight in his hands, and he asks Jesus and Mary and all the saints and angels in heaven to protect him and his family. I can see his silhouette if I walk past their room in the dark. I can't hear him make these requests, but I know what he's thinking. And I'm sure sometimes he silently cries. My father cries easily. He prays nightly and cries easily because he's always confronting poverty. Because his faith supersedes darkness. One decade each weekday night. On Sundays he prays all five of them.

In my father's mind, having the same name as the saint who brought the rosary from heaven to earth by way of the Virgin Mary gives him an edge over the rest of the world, and God knows my father could definitely use an edge. Seven hundred years before my father was born, Saint Dominic withdrew to a forest to pray and the Virgin Mary appeared. She taught him the rosary and told him to teach it to the rest of the world, which he did, and he became a saint. And for as long as those black beads slip through my father's fingers, there is some form of comfort from the trials of this world.

Mitch Miller is finishing "The Yellow Rose of Texas" downstairs in the kitchen, and a man guarantees everyone within listening range that Rinso will produce a bright, sweet-smelling wash every time.

Wash, dress, make the bed, pray. Move the cushions. Check the new flowers in the jar. Turn them around so the other side gets a day in the sun.

Down the stairs, past Saint Francis, and into the kitchen. My aunt is buttering toast and "Love Is a Many-Splendored Thing" is filling the room. My uncle is gone for his day at the store.

Ever since the hamlet came into being, men have gone off to work in the morning. They've worked in the forest at sawmills for weeks at a time. Dried their clothes near a stove made from an oil drum. Once in a while, a chaplain would visit a camp on a Sunday. He'd read the Bible and they'd sing a few hymns.

Men work as miners, or fish from a schooner for weeks. Men deliver cartons of eggs that are perfect. Or they walk down a road, turn a key in the front door of a store, flick a few switches, and flip a sign that says CLOSED back to OPEN. Or, like my father, they get into a blue Chevrolet—its trunk packed with boxes of cookies and paint, and its glove compartment filled with small chips of colour—and head off to outports and towns, filling dozens of orders.

The boys aren't awake, and my aunt brings our plates to the table. Sign of the cross and breakfast.

We talk about school. I don't mention blisters from straps. We talk about home. I don't mention my mother's affliction. I don't mention my bumpless head or the butcher knife or the cursing. I don't mention much about what's really going on in my life. We talk about the two boys and my time in the hamlet. About Matilda. The shoreline. The four deer I saw in the rain.

Even though she's religious, I don't mention that I'm praying a minimum of twelve times a day, sometimes fourteen. I wonder how often she prays. I pray when I get up in the morning, before and after breakfast, when we arrive in school, before we leave for lunch, before and after lunch, when we get back to school after lunch, when we leave school at the end of the day, before and after supper, and before I go to bed. And that doesn't include Sundays and feast days, which seem to be daily. I'm praying as much as a nun. If there isn't a thought revolving around in my mind, I'm praying to Jesus and Mary and wondering whether, if he returns, Jesus will be as compassionate this time around.

I don't mention the fainting spells. That I get dizzy in school, and dizzy making my bed. That I've been brought home from church twice but no one knows what's wrong with me. I faint. Someone brings me home. *Margaret fainted again.*

I ask her if she has dreams. She does, but only once in a while.

I tell her that I dream almost every night of my life.

What do you dream about, Margaret?

I can't tell her that last night I dreamt about commas.

The two boys are awake. Boil the eggs, one slice of bread in the toaster, two half glasses of milk, and the bulletin board comes on the radio. Farmers are having a display of their tractors next Saturday morning. Tennessee Ernie Ford—*you load sixteen tons, and what do you get?*

The boys are eating breakfast and my aunt's on the phone. A breeze from the bay pours through the kitchen's screen door. Chatter of birds. I make a half cup of tea for myself. "Cherry Pink and Apple Blossom White." Pat Boone—"Ain't That a Shame."

No one is yelling or screaming or slamming a door. No one is making threats. And I know life isn't perfect anywhere on the face of the earth, but there's a peacefulness here that I don't know how to explain to myself. There's something very right here and something very wrong at home with the affliction. Something wrong with the fears, and the abuse from the nuns. Something wrong with being afraid every single day of my life—except down by the bay and the field and by the spare-room window. No one in the hamlet is feeling for bumps on my head.

Finish breakfast. Out the door, through the yard, down the road to the field. Stories about spiders and rocks and things on the ground. Gulls and crows and schooners. Cobb Lane and Bonne Bay. Stories are endless. The boys have their own books and I read them, and they enjoy the stories I make up myself, so I do both.

I can't imagine a world without books, or a dictionary or atlas. Or my collection of movie magazines. My cousin only wants pages with Marilyn Monroe, so I inherit the bulk of Hollywood. Sal Mineo, Rock Hudson, and Elizabeth Taylor. *106 Things You Never Knew About Liz: She likes to write poetry. She has a Rolls-Royce, hates to make phone calls, and talks to her dogs. Her favourite dessert is lemon meringue pie. Violets and lilacs are her favourite flowers. She doesn't get along well with her mother. And she doesn't get carsick.* Her Rolls-Royce probably has enormous, long diamond chains attached to the bumper.

The only book I've ever seen my mother read is a red one. A book of poetry by Robert Burns. A red tartan cover and pages edged with real gold. It's her book and nobody touches it. It lives in the bookcase.

When we moved into town, my father built a brick and plank bookcase along three sides of the living-room wall. Built the entire thing in one day—he wanted to get it done. And my mother arranged the books by colour—a grid of pigment-identified literature. Burns lives at the end of the reds.

I have my own library card and can read about Burns whenever I want to. And except for the occasional sound of bowling pins crashing on walls, the library is quiet, and a person can do a great deal of reading.

Burns named his first child Elizabeth. He fell into long bouts of depression just like my mother. He called it *bouts with the demons,* which is exactly what my mother would call it if she had a name for the affliction. He was a farmer and plunged a shovel into the earth. He loved flowers and he was Scottish. It was a match made in heaven.

The boys get comfortable. The blanket, a snack for the morning, the view of the bay from the field, schooners and gulls.

Now, did you ever hear a story like this one? I begin like my uncle. The two-year-old won't understand, but the three-year-old may ask an interesting question.

This is the story of Shanawdithit, the very last Beothuk. The Beothuk lived in Newfoundland for thousands of years and kept to themselves. Some of them lived right here in the hamlet. I pause for a few seconds, like my uncle.

They built wigwams and wore cloaks made from caribou skins in the winter. In summer they fished and in winter they moved inland to hunt.

Then the Europeans arrived and took all the fish and thousands of Beothuk starved.

In 1811, exactly one hundred years before my father was born, there was a great search to find a Beothuk, but not one was found. Then one day, trappers found three starving Beothuk women—a mother and her two daughters. They were brought to a doctor, but they were sick with tuberculosis and the mother and one daughter died. But one daughter lived. Shanawdithit. And she was put to work as a servant. People think she was about twenty-two years old.

I unwrap the cookies.

It's 1828. A kind Newfoundland researcher, William Cormack, hears about Shanawdithit and brings her home to his family. She draws pictures of her own people, and their houses and tools and clothing, and their battles with Europeans, and things from her childhood.

She translates words from her language into English. She's graceful, intelligent, and especially good with children. She becomes a great friend to Cormack's family. But in less than a year, Cormack has to leave Newfoundland, and Shanawdithit gives him the only two things that she owns—a piece of quartz from the Newfoundland earth and a lock of her hair.

I stop there.

That's the story. She gave Cormack two gifts.

Why?

Because she wanted to give him a gift.

Why?

I can't tell them the rest.

Six months after Cormack leaves, Shanawdithit dies of tuberculosis just like her mother and sister did, and the doctor cuts off her head and sends it to London so doctors can study it. The rest of her is buried in a Newfoundland graveyard for people who don't belong to a church—people who are probably going to limbo anyway and won't be needing their heads.

I think Shanawdithit went directly to heaven, where her head was quickly returned—because everything is made right in heaven. That's the true story of Shanawdithit. After all she'd been through, they cut off her head.

Up the road, into the house. Soup, cookie, milk. Wash up, down the road, past whitewashed fences and houses, past Matilda, who's not on the porch or out in her yard. Maybe she's at the back of the house in the vegetable garden, with her hands in the very best soil. My mother will be in her garden all afternoon, moving her hands like a plough around the base of the beautiful peonies. If a cluster of feathers could be a flower, it would be a peony. Then she'll go back inside, put on the kettle, have a cup of hot tea, a few sample cookies, and then rest on the back porch and view the fruits of her labour. Asters, grape hyacinths, phlox. Pansy and forget-me-not borders. A row of sweet peas. Poppies and mums. Foxgloves and sweet williams—*Fire Engine Red.* Something is always in bloom, winding itself around rocks. And she'll be keeping track of the front door and back. She'll be on the back porch—she just came out through the back door. It's bad luck to come in one door and leave by another on the same day, so she has to keep track. If she has to go into town, she has to leave by the back door. A ringing in her left ear means bad news is coming—but she'll know that already.

She'll be at peace for the moment, away from demons hiding inside the house or waiting up on the roof. It's the only time in her life that she escapes them. The only time I escape them myself. She'll enjoy her tea and take long puffs on her cigarette—filtered, the safe kind—and she'll have the radio on low in the kitchen. Relaxing music. A daytime drama. Frank Sinatra, Vera Lynn, and Nat King Cole. A special report for housewives—personal and household advice. A Newfoundland folk song.

She's like the swallow that flies so high,
She's like the river that never runs dry,
She's like the sunshine on the lee shore,
I love my love and love is no more.

All the women are out in their gardens. Mrs. Clark is with a flurry of hens and their feathers are floating down through the air and landing on top of her dahlias. And Miss Mary Cobb's garden is whatever God happened to put on the ground when the universe was being created that day. It's probably exactly the same as it was eight million years ago, except for the telephone pole.

The man with the trellis is standing inside his gate, clipping and eyeing the hedge, making it perfect.

How are ye gettin' on, my dear?

I tell him everything's good.

That's grand, my dear. No point in being in a hobble about anything.

As long as there's a Newfoundland, someone will be asking me if I'm gettin' on okay.

Pray, supper, pray. Help with the dishes. Help put the two boys to bed.

My uncle is smoking his cigar on the porch, comfortable in a wide garden chair.

A few people are taking a Friday night stroll and children are running and laughing before they slow down for the night. Smell of evening—salt water and flowers. Evening wind. My aunt's on the telephone, listening to someone who's doing most of the talking.

Mary Cobb and my mother talk on the phone in the late afternoon. They have long chats about weather or damage to a section of rail. The price of salt cod. Relatives, or who's having a baby. I listen to my mother's side of the conversation and try to imagine a woman brave enough to live alone in the woods, without electricity, neighbours, or even a road. If she breaks her own bone, she probably knows how to repair it.

Mary Cobb endures complete isolation if trains can't get through or phone lines are down. She lives in a house buried in snow for days at a time—puffs of blue chimney smoke marking her place in the world. Her life in the woods is beyond Katharine Hepburn or Scarlett O'Hara. Beyond Bette Davis. Beyond, beyond. A woman in a plain cotton dress with a cup of hot tea. A woman alone in the woods feeding chickens.

Since I can never get enough of the bay and the shore and I don't know if I'll ever be back here again on my own, I take a handful of cookies and head back to the water.

Stillness. Salty wind on my face. Gulls and sound of the waves. Someone says, *How are ye gettin' on, my dear?* and I say *Good!* because it's true.

I'll probably have the occasional blank look on my face no matter how long I live. Will still have slightly pigeon-toed feet and unreadable bumps.

And even though there may be chaos everywhere else on the face of this earth—even though there may be no escape from life in a house with my mother's affliction, or escape from the nuns who think they're one step away from being Jesus himself—there's still one reliable, reachable place of serenity almost every day of my life.

In summer, Cobb Lane is quiet with its flowers, white swans, and pond, but in winter, with its massive blanket of white and its often below-zero temperatures, there's complete and utter tranquility. Snow covers bare branches of trees and walkways vanish. The earth and everything on it is sleeping.

It's a proliferation of colour and blossoms in summer, but in winter it's a proliferation of starkness. An exquisite light-filled world of simplicity. Bleached white snowdrifts as blinding as searchlights. A silver-white sky so heavy with snow you can see its weight in the clouds. My footsteps make soft squeaking sounds as I walk past snow-covered yards. Trees rock slowly and snow falls on my head like a blessing. On Cobb Lane in winter, things are so quiet that even the swans are asleep. They're safe in a swan house, where they're cared for until the warm winds of spring. The landscape and everything nature has ever produced—trees, mountains, and ground—is a vista of white. *White as the pure driven snow.*

The Beothuk probably walked on Cobb Lane. How did I arrive here in place of the Beothuk? Count it!

They lived on the island for thousands of years. They were living here when the Vikings arrived. The Vikings called the Beothuk *the skraelings, the barbarians.* A strange choice of words considering the source. The Vikings left Newfoundland after three or four years. Life was too harsh and winters too cold and the Beothuk were probably happy to see them sail back to Greenland. Then came Queen Elizabeth I and Sir Humphrey Gilbert and the explorers and pirates and hundreds of ships and thousands of fishermen off the Newfoundland coast and the eradication of every single Beothuk that ever lived on the island. In 1829, the last surviving Beothuk, Shanawdithit, died of tuberculosis, like her mother and sister before her. It was the end of the Beothuk nation. Extermination. Then settlements, and wars between the French and the English, and England claiming Newfoundland as its own private territory, and Pop leaving Lebanon and selling dry goods along the Labrador coast from the schooner. And in 1897, exactly nine hundred years after the Vikings, Miss Mary Cobb was born. Then the very first radio message was sent across the Atlantic from England to Newfoundland. And ten years later, in 1911, my father was born. And the island never recovered after the Great Depression, and it joined Canada in 1949, and my father lost his store and our home and we lived in the woods for two years and finally saved enough money to move back into town, and here I am on Cobb Lane, on the snow-covered earth, and all the Beothuk are gone and all the gardens are white.

Tall stalks of brown vegetation pierce the drifts like aboriginal spears. Blackbirds criss-cross a grey winter sky and sparrows fly wherever they please. Pieces of broken twigs like broken lines across white. Warm curtains on windows. Shovelled paths, and wreaths of twigs and berries on doors. Chimney smoke curling its way from rooftop to sky. The hedges are brown, as if the green has been sucked right into the earth, but then in spring the green miraculously rises up from the ground. Maybe that's why it's called spring.

In winter the pond is a wide sweeping rink. Small children struggle with their first pair of skates and teenagers glide around them. People make long skating chains by holding each other's coattails.

On Cobb Lane, for one half hour, I'm not afraid for my life. No one is banging the top of my head or blocking the doors with bureaus. I'm not down on my knees, repenting in Latin because I'm living in sin with a Presbyterian woman who won't stop cursing.

All week I've tried to describe Cobb Lane to the two boys, but the three-year-old is distracted by crows now that he's pointing and counting, and the two-year-old asks *Why?* but I can't explain why Cobb Lane is important. I tell them stories about walks in a forest and spiders. About the Beothuk and how they built forts of their own, right here in the hamlet. How their children played in the snow, picked blueberries, splashed in the water, and watched shooting stars before going into the wigwam at night.

A pale early moon hangs over the bay and the hamlet tonight. Pink evening light fills the sky. Gulls are screeching and diving and pecking through driftwood and shells, their long beaks poking through sand. Their dinner just arrived from the ocean and washed up on the rocks.

If I walked from the very beginning to the very end of the beach, every one of those rocks would be as smooth as oil—every edge worn down by the sea.

People are having a snack by the water. A blanket, cookies, glass jars with tea.

What kind of cookie would you like, my dear?

Don't make a particle of difference, girl. They're all delicious.

Up the road, past the trellis, past my uncle's store and the church. Back to the house. Tea and toast with my aunt and uncle. *Now, did you ever hear a story like this one?* and my uncle starts up with a yarn.

Up the stairs, move the three pillows, look through the window. There's another white cloud that looks like a road, except now there are more of them. In houses with lights, people are gathered downstairs—probably having their own cup of hot tea and piece of warm toast around their own kitchen table.

The bay is a piece of shimmering dark blue and black, with white light from the moon. The breeze is warm on my face, and from where I stand in the world at this moment—a spare-room window overlooking a hamlet and bay, rectangles of brown and green earth, long, cream-coloured clouds and a very dark sky, stars in the millions, curtains barely stirring, moonlight on trees and water—I see only beauty. A hamlet at night. People sleeping. As if the hamlet has closed its own eyes. For the most part, people feel safe, and I wonder why people would want to live anywhere else.

I feel as if I'm almost in half. Somewhere between my mother's affliction and the calm of the hamlet. Halfway between the picture of night that I see for myself and the horror my mother has trapped in her mind. I'm standing on one of those treacherous, beautiful roads in the sky.

I look through the window and watch until I can't stay awake anymore.

Chapter Eight

SATURDAY *Day Eight*

The morning view from the spare-room window is a view I'll keep in my mind forever. The wide open sky and road in front of the house. The slight incline. Not an incline enough to be considered a hill—not even enough to get a sled started in winter—but an incline. The glossy grey and white seagulls. The shimmering, silver, changeable bay. The smell of freshly cut grass and flowers beside all the whitewashed fences and barns. The houses with porches and brightly painted screen doors. The two large plots in my aunt's garden with dahlias, delphiniums, and something tiny and white. And how everything under that wide open sky is exactly the same during the night as it is during the day, except for the light. It changes everything.

My mother sees something petrifying every night of her life. Something evil hiding in shadows. Something outside the windows or outside the door. She hears ominous sounds. A moaning, groaning wind—a wind that's known nothing but trouble. Something waiting to harm her. She looked exceedingly happy before I was born, smiling in black-and-white photos. Fishing trips and picnics with friends. Or dressed in a fine coat, with earrings and makeup. Something changed her and I don't know if it was me, but it's difficult to believe I came into this world just to provoke her. I don't know if she banged doors and was afraid of the dark when she was young, but if I really stare at her picture—if I stare at her photograph and look right into her eyes—I can almost see the affliction.

Last night I dreamt I was running through a small, dimly lit house. It was night in my dream and a note in my mother's handwriting was taped to a door. I said *Oh God* and put the note in my pocket without reading it. I was overwhelmed with fear and kept running, and I woke up in the middle of running. I wasn't running anywhere in particular. I was just running.

It's my second-last day in a room filled with everything red. The afghan. Jesus in the red plastic frame over the bed. Roses on the hooked rug. The breeze is cool and moves through the bedroom like waves. It covers my face and shoulders. The floorboards are cold. I forgot to bring my slippers. Beep of a horn. Woof of a dog. Sound of birds in a chirping, feeding frenzy.

Voices of people outside on the street.

How's she gettin' on, b'y?

Best kind, b'y. It's gonna be a hot one I think.

Yes, b'y. The sun'll be splittin' the rocks before ya know it.

No argument out of me, b'y.

It's Saturday morning and a few children are racing around even though it's not even seven o'clock.

Children in hamlets, for the most part, live an exceedingly different life from children in cities. Berry picking in summer, walks by the tracks, or fishing. In winter, when the harbour is frozen and snow has fallen, they skate on homemade rinks—blurs of colour circle wide open space like Newfoundland tundra. The boys all play hockey, with a stick and a puck, or a piece of wood to masquerade as a puck. If their families can't afford skates, they attach blades to their boots.

In hamlets, the Christmas pageant is always the same. The same volunteer parent organizes Joseph and Mary and angels and shepherds and the young child dressed as a lamb and is also the narrator, and is always a wreck. Angels will leave their heavenly post and wander the aisles, and people won't know whether to laugh or cry, so they'll do both.

These days in the hamlet have been a chance to think in a way I've never been able to think in all eleven years of my life. A chance to have conversations I've never even dreamt about having. To meet people I never knew I'd be meeting.

Wash, dress, pray. Move the three massive pillows for the second-last time. Down the stairs and into the kitchen.

My aunt brings two plates to the table and they're identical—a fried egg, two strips of bacon, and two slices of hot buttered toast. I'd like to tell her about Freddie, who was our boarder when we first moved into town from the woods, but then I'd have to explain the affliction, so it's better to keep things to myself.

Freddie had a unique way of eating. He'd wrap whatever my mother served him for breakfast inside his toast, then dip the entire package into his tea. Sausages, eggs, hot buttered toast—inside the cup. Sausage grease floating on milk. Five or six bites and he'd be gone. It was completely disgusting and such a waste of good food. It would've taken me half an hour to devour that much food, if I'd had it.

Just say you've eaten, is what my mother would say just before my father and Freddie came home for supper. *Just say you've eaten.* And there was always something—an egg, a piece of bread with Cheese Whiz, or a piece of blood pudding. Blood pudding is exactly what it sounds like except for the pudding.

My father and Freddie would come home at the end of the day and my father would say, *Where's your supper?*

I've already eaten.

On Sundays we all ate the same.

My aunt pours the tea and the Saturday morning bulletin board comes on the radio. There'll be a penny social organized by the Knights of Columbus. A community dance. News of the world: The Suez Canal. Threats of attacks and invasions. Joey Smallwood making another government deal. News about cod and capelin. News of Grace Kelly and the Prince of Monaco. News of an Alberta murder—John Etter Clark, a teacher, farmer, and politician. His wife's name was Margaret. Clark murdered Margaret, their son and three daughters, a hired hand, and a visitor. He shot all seven right through the head. A neighbour discovered the bodies. The Mounties found Clark dead in the woods. He'd shot himself through the head.

If my mother is hearing this now, she's probably in a petrified state as she sits in the kitchen finishing breakfast or reading her leaves, and the leaves are surely spelling disaster. She's probably looking right at the phone.

It's November 1955. Less than a year ago. Almost midnight. My mother's bedroom. Curtains are pinned all the way down, the keyhole is plugged with a face cloth, and a folded blanket is at the foot of the door to prevent any demon that may be on the other side of the door from looking under. A bureau is blocking the door and there's a tin pot in the corner, if needed. No one can enter or leave the room and my mother has the blanket over her head.

There's a nightstand on my father's side of the bed—a lamp in the centre and an area below with a door where there never seems to be anything. In some homes this is where you'd store the revolver, but we don't have anything that resembles a weapon, except for the butcher knife in the kitchen.

My father is travelling treacherous roads, with snow chains attached to the tires and Christmas tree jellies, ribbon candy, and elaborate boxes of chocolates packed in the trunk. November is an opportunity for enormous sales.

On most nights my father would be in bed with my mother, but tonight the protector is me. I don't know who's responsible for my well-being. Hopefully Jesus or Mary, or the enormous angel in a long flowing gown who helps children cross hazardous bridges.

The view from the bedroom window, when it's visible, is the upper limbs of the two poplar trees by the gate and two spinsters who live directly across the street and spend their lives close to the glass. They sit in the living room during the day, watching the street and with it the neighbours, which in this case is us. At night they sit in the dark and spy through the curtains as if no one knows where they are. The street lamp in front of the house gives them away. The spinsters are the town cavalry—the only things missing are bugles and horses.

It's almost midnight and the sound of stones hitting the bedroom window wakes me. A slow, repetitive sound, like rain on a roof. I look at my mother. Her eyes are wide and staring and she's got a petrified look on her face.

The number of stones hitting the window increases, so I slide out of bed and crawl to the window. Lawrence, my cousin, is down on the sidewalk and I open the curtain just enough to let him know that I'm there. Lawrence is fifteen and tall for his age and light from the street lamp is giving him an eerie blue glow. He's waving frantically for me to come downstairs.

I turn to my mother. *I think something's happened. Lawrence is down by the gate and he's waving frantically.*

She throws the blanket into the air as if it's on fire. A sliver of light penetrates the gap in the curtains. We push the bureau away from the door. She reaches to her neck for a key on a string, removes the face cloth that's plugging the keyhole, shoves the blanket away from the foot of the door, pushes the key into the hole, and turns it. She braces herself and we go down the stairs, hems of our nightgowns scraping the floor, bare feet on the cold plastic runner.

We push armchairs away from the front door. She removes another face cloth jamming another keyhole, produces a key that was hidden beneath a begonia, unlocks the door, and lets Lawrence inside.

Oh my God, Lawrence says. *Something terrible happened at Harry's Brook.* And with that we move to the kitchen. Whenever something happens, we move to the kitchen.

Lawrence dials the RCMP and they explain things to my mother and the chrome on the stove reflects the utterly horrified look on her face. I lean on the wall, silent except for my breathing. How did I get to this moment? Count it!

First, my mother attended a small non-Catholic school. Reading, arithmetic, writing, and spelling. In winter, children brought wood for the stove. She finished grade ten, volunteered at the hospital, worked in a store, and met my father, the Lebanese Roman Catholic. They went on fishing trips and picnics with friends—they both loved the outdoors. She and my father married and in 1944, during the Second World War, I entered the world one thousand years after the Vikings, right to the day. Now, eleven years later, I'm in the kitchen and the affliction is mirrored in chrome. There's only one thing to do. I stare at the chrome.

Miss Mary Cobb and her sister, my mother's mother, who just happened to be visiting Harry's Brook, have been savagely beaten into unconsciousness and the attacker is on the loose.

This being the situation, no one goes back to bed and every light bulb in the house is turned on. If a door wasn't fully blocked before, it is now—and with very heavy furniture. The basement door is secured with the kitchen table and curtains are pinned all the way down. We're thoroughly barricaded inside the kitchen, and the telephone rings. It's the spinsters, wanting to know.

It's mid-October—just a few weeks before the attack. A John Sutton is working in a lumber camp near Gallants, eight miles from Miss Mary Cobb. He has a reputation for being a thief, has a criminal record, and hears the legend that Mary Cobb has money hidden in trunks. Anyone who knows her knows it's a lie.

End of October. He finishes his job at the camp, goes to the nearest town—which is ours—and rents a room at a boarding house that is, by coincidence, a short walk from our house. *A gunshot away.*

I'm in grade six with the nuns and on my knees praying for savages, Communists, and Presbyterians. There's a cardboard pumpkin on a wall in the hallway.

On Thursday morning, 3 November, Sutton returns to Gallants in a taxi and ducks down in the back to avoid being seen, walks the eight miles on the tracks to Mary Cobb's house, and hides in the woods, concealed behind branches. His view is a well, rainwater barrels, a ladder, a broom, a shovel, an axe.

It's late afternoon. Mary Cobb opens the door, throws feed to the chickens, and goes back inside. Sutton creeps to the house holding a large jagged rock. The door opens again, Mary Cobb steps outside, and Sutton strikes her head with the rock, beats her head with the broom handle, then grabs the axe handle and beats her until she's unconscious. He looks at the blood-soaked body, forgets about money, and runs to the tracks.

Mary Cobb's sister hears the screaming, looks through the window, sees the attack, calls the police, and screams that she's Mary Cobb's sister and to come immediately because Miss Mary Cobb has been murdered.

Sutton is racing across the yard, looks back at the house, sees a woman's face in the window, grabs a large heavy rock, runs back to the house, across the porch, and into the hallway, lunges at Mary Cobb's sister, and with the force of a lumberjack, beats her until she's unconscious. He grabs money from inside a handbag, runs past the two bodies and up to the tracks.

It's just after school. I'm on Cobb Lane, away from pathological nuns, away from the affliction and swearing. Yards are a seamless blanket of new-fallen snow. I stand on the embankment. The swans are gone and November is cold. I'm on my way home.

Around six o'clock, Sutton runs from the woods, sees three boys near the tracks, tells them he needs a taxi, and the boys take him to the home of a driver. Sutton hires the man to take him to a town with a boat to the mainland. They stop for a meal at Sutton's request and expense, and Sutton buys snacks for the one-hundred-mile trip.

It's early evening and I'm doing homework up in my room. My mother is reading her leaves, and my father is somewhere on an icy road with samples of cookies, Christmas candy, and house paint.

The Mounties, a doctor, and a railroad speeder crew arrive at Mary Cobb's house. The only light is a small fire in the stove and the table is set for a meal. The blood-soaked axe handle is next to Mary Cobb's head. A large, blood-covered rock is near her sister. Both bodies are soaked with blood. The Mounties radio the telegraph operator, who radios a wood train nearby, and it speeds to Harry's Brook, brings the unconscious women to the area hospital—half an hour away—and roadblocks are set up in every direction. Every train and car is searched.

In the morning, police question people who live near the tracks, the boys tell their story, the driver is questioned, their description is radioed across Newfoundland, and the RCMP, working with the description, find Sutton waiting for a boat to the mainland.

Not that my mother ever needed it once in her life, but now she has proof of the devil, and they may have chatted if he happened to walk past our house while he contemplated his crime. They may have spoken as she weeded the dahlias.

Mary Cobb remains unconscious for nine days. Her sister remains unconscious for five. Mary Cobb's sister is seventy-three years of age. Mary Cobb is fifty-eight.

Mary Cobb's sister was beaten so badly her memory is severed forever, and Mary Cobb has been beaten almost to death. She needs someone to offer care and protection, and as fate would allow it, that protector is my mother. It's an unlikely combination—Mary Cobb being a broken and shattered woman, and my mother being herself.

During the winter, except for Mary Cobb's slow but steady improvement, most things remain exactly the same. Strappings continue because we've done terrible things, or may do terrible things, or did terrible things in the past, and if we're strapped often enough we'll stop making so many mistakes. Either way, we're all doomed.

I still have the tragic look on my face, but I don't have to walk with a book on my head anymore because the nuns have given up on me completely. My father travels the outport roads but he gets so many orders he has to do arithmetic at the dining-room table and there's a fatigue at the end of the week that weighs on his eyes.

Sutton gets a fourteen-year sentence. It's by the slimmest of margins that he wasn't charged with multiple murders.

Mary Cobb learns to walk once again and, in the spring, takes the train back to her home in the Newfoundland wilderness. Rail workers carry her bags from the train to the house. They'd been safeguarding her home while she healed, and she probably whispered *Blessed be my friends who move on the rails.* Miss Mary Cobb is beyond Katharine Hepburn. She's beyond Hollywood, beyond any movie. She's beyond, beyond!

My aunt fills the two cups, returns the teapot to the ceramic tile on top of the stove, turns the radio down, and "The Ballad of Davy Crockett" disappears almost before it begins—*king of the wild frontier.* The boys are awake and this is my last full day in the hamlet. Butter the toast, cut the eggs, orange juice in a cup, *Down the chute.* Wash up, out the door, down the steps, out the gate, down the road to Matilda and she's out in the yard, just as I'd hoped she would be, and she sees me, just as I'd hoped she would, and she waves me into the yard with her big *Come on in* kind of wave, and I stop by the gate. If she'd stayed in the outport, I would never have met her.

I 'ear you're leaving, my dear.

How do they know?

She holds out a small box tied with a ribbon. *I know you like going down by the shore, my dear. It's so you don't completely forget me.*

How can I forget someone named Waltzing Matilda? It's tiny shells from the beach strung on a cord.

You've done a good job with the boys and that's as true as the gospel, my luv. True as the gospel. Come back again soon. You're as welcome as the angels in 'eaven, my luv.

I say thank you and give her a hug and she hugs the two boys and I wish I could put her right in my pocket and keep her with me forever.

It's my last day by the shore—by the splashing and lapping of water, the gulls screaming and soaring, the woods by the side of the road. My last walk beside long rows of vegetables protected by chicken-wire netting and all the whitewashed fences and barns, and people saying *How are ye gettin' on, my dear? How are ye gettin' on?*

The boys are pointing at crows, the gulls are screeching, and I hug Matilda again and head for the field. The boys couldn't care less that I've been in charge of them for over a week. All they want is their fill of stories and walks to the field and beyond.

In the evening, there's a cloud over the hamlet that's as large as the sky. It hovers in all directions like an enormous floating roof, a thickness of pink and silver and blue. It makes the hamlet look as small as a thimble. It looks like it could open its mouth and swallow everyone here, and if it weren't so exquisitely beautiful it would be utterly frightening. Mr. Clark would say, *Well, by the hole in my coat. Now that's a cloud.* And there's a cloud in my mind when I think of that now, and how everything happened so quickly.

It's only eight weeks ago. Almost the end of the day. Almost the end of grade six and my father's home from work early. Our news of the day comes from the small black radio on a corner shelf in the kitchen, or from my father after work. Tonight he doesn't even stop to remove his rubbers or wipe his feet on the mat. He heads straight for the kitchen.

My good God Almighty. Poor Jim Clark was drowned last night.

My mother drops the spatula. *Oh for Christ's sake!*

I was just getting into the car. One of the guys yells out at me, "Did you hear about poor Jim Clark?" Drowned when he was doing a friend a favour. What a damn, damn crime. I can't believe it. God Almighty. I'll tell you one thing: if there's an angel in heaven tonight, it's got Jim Clark's name on it. What a damn crime.

My mother says *Oh for Christ's sake* again. It's all she can say.

I stand between the two of them, both of them swearing. My father stands in the kitchen doorway and my mother stands next to the stove and I've never heard my father swear once in his life and all I can do is stand there. All I can think is *Well, by the hole in my coat* and Mr. Clark driving me to school in the early morning with a truck filled with perfect eggs for his customers who wanted perfection. Mr. Clark who loved every story I ever told him. Couldn't wait to hear the things that had happened. Couldn't believe all the things that I knew. *Well, by the hole in my coat, Margaret.*

Jim was covering a shift for a buddy—some kind of emergency with one of his children. My father is talking strangely, his voice is choking, and he keeps wiping his eyes with his hankie. My mother listens and keeps repeating *Oh for Christ's sake.*

The fellow needed a few hours off and Jim offered to help him out and cover the shift. Can you imagine what must be going through that fellow's mind?

I can't understand, but I'm listening. Something to do with a logging boat and a large anchor over the bow, a large boom of logs, chains, and boom timbers, and pushing logs in the mill's direction and cable winding and something snapping and a crashing wave and the boat tipping into the cold dark water and Mr. Clark in his thick jacket and boots was thrown over the side and had no chance of swimming and sank to the bottom under the logs.

They talk about Mrs. Clark. *How will she cope? Who'll take care of her now? How will she manage? You never know when it's going to happen. You just never know. Good God Almighty. What a damn crime. What a damn, damn crime.*

And all I'm wondering is what Jesus and God had in mind when they made this happen last night. What did Jesus have in his mind? *What were you thinking, Jesus? What were you thinking?* Mr. Clark was the kindest person I've ever known in my life. And it would be just like him to give up his life for a friend, especially a friend with children.

Mr. Clark is drowned and gone and Mary Genesius who is nothing but hatred and evil is alive in the convent. I will never understand God's sense of justice if I live to be eighty.

Mr. Clark was laid to rest and it was one of the saddest days of my life and one I'll never forget. If the birds were singing, I don't know why. They should have known better.

Chapter Nine

SUNDAY, *Day Nine*

It's Sunday and we'll be driving back to the halfway point after lunch.

Last night in my dream I was listening to a woman talk about Creation as she was making a pot of tea and I was trying to follow along. She turned to me and said, *You don't know what I'm talking about, do you?* I said *No.*

She said, *Look at the painting.*

A huge painting appeared before me with a sunlit meadow, hills, and trees. Light shimmered on grass and flowers. There seemed to be stars in the sky even though it was daytime. A large group of people stood around in a loose circle and they were glowing. A beam of light was shining up from the ground as if it were part of the earth. There'd been a question-and-answer period and she said I'd asked some very good questions. I decided to make a cup of tea for myself, but I woke up.

There are no lawn mowers or trucks hauling things. No shouting voices. Only quiet. The hamlet windows are golden rectangles reflecting the sun, and if someone is looking up at the spare-room window right now, they'll see a glowing rectangle with my face and possibly bumpless head right in the centre.

The sky over the hamlet is the same exact sky that's over our house, over enormous Hollywood mansions, and over the unbaptized children in Africa living in their grass huts. It's the same exact sky that existed over the earliest home in the hamlet.

How did I get from the earliest home in the hamlet to the spare-room window on Sunday morning? Count it!

The first people lived in wigwams and kept to themselves. Then invaders, schooners, seal nets, and cod traps. Steamers, railways, and mills to make paper. People cleared land and grew fields of oats and potatoes. They built fences and homes, a school, and a church. Church was the glue that held people together. And before they had churches they attended Mass in somebody's home, or right in Pop's store. Priests travelled by schooner and endured treacherous storms on the Atlantic. But now there's a church just up the road, less than ten minutes away, with pews and statues and lace on the altar, and the priest doesn't have to endure a treacherous ocean—he just has to buy gas for the car and make sure he has a medallion.

Make the bed. Pray. Move the pillows for the very last time. Down the stairs and skip breakfast since it's before Communion. Hello to my uncle—it's his turn to stay home with the boys.

Sounds of a church service are filling the kitchen. A non-Catholic radio service. A choir, an organ, and a non-Catholic hymn—"Rock of Ages." But the house is filled with the sounds of a choir, even though it's a non-Catholic one.

Out the door, through the gate, and up the road to the Catholic church.

After Mass, most of the morning is spent gathering my things, although I only have the one suitcase. I can wear the straw hat so I don't have to pack it. I change out of the good clothes and good shoes, pack the stones and shells I've been collecting since I arrived, and put the stolen pebble deep in my pocket. Leave the flowers in the glass jar or take them? I haven't decided.

Before lunch, I take the two boys for our very last walk down to the field and beyond. I'll miss the field and my uncle's store—the yellow plastic shades on the windows, the people who work there, the baskets of ribbons and trim. I'll miss the stories I make up for the boys and finding answers for some of the *Why* questions. I'll miss Waltzing Matilda and friends whose names I don't know. I'll miss people's gardens, the whitewashed sheds and fences, and whitewashed buildings. My uncle's yarns. I'll miss the place in the woods where I saw the four deer. The wild blueberry patches. Wide open gates. I'll miss the old stone chapel and the chipped statue of Mary behind the door. The children skipping and chanting as they take turns with the rope—*The King of England went to France to teach the children how to dance.* I'll miss the endless clotheslines criss-crossing the yards.

There's an order to hanging clothes on a line. Blankets and sheets go first, then all the way down to hankies and ribbons. It all narrows down to a point.

I'll miss the reading room upstairs in the drugstore, and the post office in back of the hardware store. In the hamlet, buildings have multiple functions. I'll miss the clover and myrtle and fern and the trestle covered with vines. The railroad tracks. Dandelion seeds floating like snow. The bay—ten minutes away—and its blue, wrinkled surface, which shimmers like rhinestones at times. A sky clear as blue crystal and streaked with slashes of pink. Bay, fields, mountains, and sky. A whitewashed hamlet. Kind people. This is the view I'll remember.

A man on a small garden tractor rides through the field and nods good morning. He's around the same age as my uncle, with heavy blue overalls, a heavy grey work shirt, and heavy grey gloves. His sleeves are rolled up to his elbows and his arms are tanned and weathered. He looks like he's been working outdoors all his life. I've seen him before, taking care of the field in the evening, and taking care of the gardens in front of some buildings. He stops, leans over the wheel, and smiles.

So, I hear you're leaving us!

I don't have to tell anyone anything.

Well, my dear, may you have a featherbed in heaven. You've done a good job with the two boys. You can cut a notch in the beam anytime.

I thank him for the compliment.

We talk about his work taking care of the field and the gardens around the hamlet. He takes care of the gardens in front of the Catholic church, the Anglican church, and the Salvation Army. He's either Catholic or non-Catholic, but I'm not asking. He talks about the heavy downpour during the week, and the winds. Trees lost branches and limbs were stripped of their leaves. He talks about trees as if they're his friends. He lost eight trees last winter. Some will return. Some are lost forever. He points to a large spruce at the end of the field. An enormous branch hangs like a broken arm and the inside is exposed. I can see the pink wood.

Wind shook the trees, he says, until they nearly swept the mud. And young branches snapped. But the roots go about their business of living and every spring, new branches appear.

Trees have been doing that, my luv, since the very start of day one.

The hamlet is the only home he's ever known in his life. He was born here, he says, just a few houses away, and he'll die here, by God. He's just like Miss Mary Cobb. He wants good people to care for the place when he's gone—people who won't abuse it. He says some people are just born abusers. *Whoever knit them wasted their yarn!* Three silent crows rise above trees, then down and out of sight.

I ask him about the abandoned chapel.

Well, my luv, he begins, *it was once a little chapel for priests who lived in the area. It isn't used anymore, but no one wanted to tear the thing down. No one had the heart to do it.*

A city group—he doesn't say which city—comes to the hamlet for one week every summer. They clean the chapel, light a fire in the stone fireplace, and pray. He says they're either Chinese or Polish. He can't remember which.

The chapel is abandoned for fifty-one weeks every year, and like anything that gets abandoned, there's dust. I finger the stolen pebble and hope he doesn't know or mind. Besides, it belongs to the Chinese or Polish and there are thousands of stones on the shore.

He knows where deer will appear in the evening. I know where they'll appear in the morning, but I don't mention the day I saw four on my own. He knows how to prime grounds for the season. Knows what to do if anything freezes. Knows flowers and trees and mountains by name.

He tips his hat. *May you have a featherbed in heaven, my dear.* Then he waves goodbye and rides into the distance. And I yell back, *May you have a featherbed in heaven!*

We leave the hamlet in my uncle's car. My aunt's in front, and I'm in back with the two boys. We meet my father and mother at the halfway point on the highway and I get out of one car and into the other and both cars turn around and head home, our blue Chevrolet dragging its chains, like a dragon.

Chapter Ten

After the Hamlet

And so I came back from the hamlet with all the memories of all the days and all the people. It's the start of July, one week after Waltzing Matilda and the two boys, and on Cobb Lane the trees are filled with blossoms. The swans are gliding on the pond's glassy surface again and their reflection is in the water—long, thin shadows of only their necks. Reflections of trees—every branch and leaf in reverse. Everything is reflecting itself.

At home, everything's pretty much exactly the same. Monsters prowl through the house and hide in dark corners. They stare through the windows at night and climb on the roof. My mother hides behind bolted doors when my father is on the road with cookies and paint chips. Face cloths in keyholes. Her anger escalates and it's the type of anger that keeps people at bay. The affliction follows me through the house and out to the street.

In daytime there's beauty—her garden in full, magnificent bloom. Each species with its own place and the place never changes. My mother—with her hands in the dirt, a thin sleeveless blouse, a pair of plaid knee-length shorts, and a shovel or spade nearby—escapes into a world of her own floral making. A feeling of safety. Control over things. Half the backyard is a blooming mound—a hill she creates every spring with soil and horse manure delivered by truck and we live with the stink for days.

The rock garden is at least five feet high in the centre and covered with blooms. Perennials, annuals, and bulbs. Delicate poppies, thin as red tissue, bow in the wind, and it's a miracle they're not snapped from their stems. Rhubarb next to the fence. Sweet smell of primrose. Something blooms from the beginning of spring until the first sign of frost.

She'll finish the housework, have a cup of tea and a few cookies—there's no end to the cookies—then take gardening tools and enter the world of her flowers. Smell of the earth on her hands—the very same earth that terrifies her at night. Tombstones and symbols of death. Shadows and noises and ghost stories that live in her mind. She views night through a world of superstitions and omens. But in daylight she digs right to its soul. Darkness is the cause of her fear and fear is the affliction and I don't know what she's afraid of, but it's everywhere.

I make a note in my mind of her rituals, hoping never to fear whatever ghost it is that she's seeing—hoping never in my life to be that afraid. And I pray to all the saints whose names I remember, *Please let me be a missionary someday, and if I can't be that, please keep me from making so many mistakes.* And I pray to God because I know the order of things. I've counted it!

God was the first one to die and organized things. Then Adam and Eve and Cain and Abel and all that. The Nativity and one enormous star. The Romans. Julius Caesar. Mary, Queen of Scots. The New World. Civil war and the First World War. Then the Great Depression. The atom bomb and black-and-white TV. Perry Como and Patti Page on the radio in the kitchen. Sunday morning music on CBC—violins and choirs in foreign languages. The street in front of our house in the evening. Millions of stars spelling out constellations across God's magnificent heaven. So I pray to that magnificent heaven.

And I pray that the affliction will end. That my mother's cursing, penetrating stares, and screaming will stop. That she'll become a Catholic—if it would help.

I make pictures down in the basement. Birchbark, flowers, and leaves dried in books. Pansies, forget-me-nots, and ferns are the best—they're flat and dry quickly. Foil wrappings from candy. Everything arranged and glued to cardboard from my father's dry-cleaner shirts. My own paste with flour and water. A beautiful floral world down in the basement, with its view of things from the window—the bottom of things. I pray to Saint Thérèse, the Little Flower, patron saint of all the dried vegetation I have in the cellar. And I hope it's not a complete mortal sin, but I pray to escape my mother's affliction someday. *Dear sweet, merciful Jesus, let us all overcome the affliction.*

Summer days are mainly the same: Up in the morning, make the bed, pray. Downstairs. Pray, breakfast, pray. Do whatever needs doing. Outdoors or down in the basement. Back to the kitchen table. Pray, eat, pray. Face the affliction. Outdoors again. Back to the house—pray, eat, pray. *The Loretta Young Show* on Sunday nights. Every time she whirls through that door in her long, flowing gown, I worry. Danny Thomas and Uncle Tonoose—and they're both Lebanese, like my father. *I've Got a Secret. Lassie.* The weather report. The fishing report. Upstairs. Pray, sleep, up again.

But the routine changes on Saturdays with weekend confession. Sit in a pew and try to come up with a list of interesting sins I've committed during the week. Enter the cramped confessional box and kneel on the low wooden step. A window slides open, the silhouette of a priest's head appears on the other side of the curtained screen, and I'm already down on my knees.

Yes, my child?

Bless me, Father, for I have sinned.

My sins are the same from one week to another, and so is the penance. I was angry. I swore.

Did you take the Lord's name in vain, my child?

No, Father. That would have changed the penance completely.

For your penance, say three Our Fathers, three Hail Marys, and three Glory Be to the Fathers.

I say *Thank you, Father,* and he closes the window.

Back to the pew, recite the penance, genuflect, out the door, down the hill, across town to the four o'clock movie. Gene Autry. Bob Hope. A western. A five-cent bar and potato chips.

I don't know what anyone else got for their penance or what type of sin they committed. My sins are always the same. It's never *Bless me, Father, for I have sinned. I robbed the Bank of Nova Scotia—twice. And I stole $10,000. And I couldn't care less because I've already purchased a schooner and I'm sailing away to the tropics.* Most of my sins are venial, but I fear going to hell for reasons that have little association with my own doing. I fear the strap—we all fear the strap. Sometimes I'll be stinging and raw where she hit me, with my hand so swollen I can't hold on to a pencil. I fear that the days with Mary Genesius and nuns like her will be without end. We're forbidden to move—only the nuns are allowed to move. I can see the shadows of their feet passing in the sunlight that spills beneath the bottom of the classroom door. Hear the click of a rosary. The swoosh of a billowing black gown. The heels of shoes clicking on wood. Can imagine a strap on the other side of the wall. If you were at the front of the room and you were getting the strap, and your hand had a cut, it wouldn't matter. If you held your hand back, the nun would say *Give me that hand, young lady,* and she'd pry your hand open, straighten the fingers, and strap you, and the cut would reopen. We're forbidden to speak. We are silent and pray and memorize.

I'll have plans for the future someday. I'll be focused like our grade five art teacher or Margot Davies on the BBC and know what to do with my life. But for the moment, I'm on Cobb Lane between our haunted house and grade seven.

I walk past the pond, the swans, and the quiet, tree-bordered gardens beneath a mosaic sky. Feel of soft ground underfoot. Sound of my breath, sound of my feet, sound of my heart. I feel determined and brave here. A place to feel calm. A place to feel respect for myself despite how others are treating me. A place to not be afraid all the time.

If I walk past our house in the evening—if I don't go inside, but keep walking farther north to the end of the street, past the Catholic graveyard, and up a slight hill—I can see stars and the Milky Way in the distance, as if I'm walking right into the sky, and if I walk far enough, and long enough, a door may open up in the clouds and I'll see inside and everything will be explained to me.

I think despite everything I'm somewhat strong for my age—somewhat brave—but I have no way to be sure. Sandy committed suicide because of a bone, and now he's dead and gone. Two years in the cabin, one year in the furnace room. Pop died and no one knows what happened to his cargo of dried goods. Mr. Clark is gone forever and it's a day I'll never forget no matter how long I live. My mother curses and sees demons and monsters at night and I sleep by her side in the dark when my father is out of town and stuff the keyholes with face cloths.

I have slightly pigeon-toed feet, a tragic look on my face, a possibly bumpless head, dizzy spells, and nosebleeds. There was the attempted murder of Miss Mary Cobb and her sister, years without much food on the table, the butcher knife, and praying twelve times a day for all the savages, babies in limbo, Russia, the Chinese Communists, and the Presbyterians. But now I'm deciding to pray for myself on Cobb Lane, under the sky and trees, just like the Beothuk.

I pray to the stars, the roots, and the mountains. To wind and weather. To the sun shining over the pond and light on the swans. Sounds of nature. This must have been how the Beothuk prayed, walking along the face of the earth, saying *Thank you.* A prayer to every insect and flower. Every wave in every river. Thank you for fire and rain and clouds. Thank you for the taste of fruit plucked from a tree. Light of the moon. This is probably how the hermits prayed, alone in their piles of rocks, pondering all the great mysteries, up to their knees in snow in the winter.

It's two weeks after the hamlet.

Despite her multiple scars, Miss Mary Cobb is living alone at Harry's Brook—the only way she would have it. At peace with her kerosene lamps, a fire in the wood stove. Mending and unravelling things. Her sister never recovered and will always remain an invalid. Sutton is twenty-four years of age and in prison for fourteen years. Mr. Clark is drowned and gone forever. My mother's affliction continues to escalate and I'm standing alone on Cobb Lane, with my back to the road, watching the swans. I'm eleven.

Part Two

Chapter Eleven

1956, October

I'm twelve years old and I can't stop praying. I'm praying in school and in church and at home and when I'm not thinking of anything else. I'm praying for every sin I've ever committed, for savages all over the world, and for non-Catholics, including my mother, who was born Presbyterian. And I say Hail Marys more than Our Fathers because Mary seems more accessible. We're reciting litanies to the Sacred Hearts of Jesus and Mary and to saints whose names are impossible to pronounce or remember. Menas Kallikelados, Jerome Emiliani, and Peregrine Laziosi—patrons of travelling merchants, orphans, and people with cancer. There's no patron saint for the poor souls trapped forever in limbo, so in addition to everything else, they're left on their own.

I dreamt about moons last night. Hundreds of moons. And they were whizzing like birds, dipping and soaring above me. I thought, in my dream, *Who will believe me? Who will ever believe me?* And I kept repeating the question as moons whizzed above me and I woke up not knowing if anyone did.

I can smell toast and fried capelin. The smell of whatever is being cooked in the kitchen drifts up through a grate in the hallway floor. There's no end to the bones in a capelin. A capelin is small, its sides are silver like a sardine, and its thousands of tiny soft bones are easier to eat than to pick over.

Into the kitchen and avoid my mother's eyes when it's possible. Avoid her world of omens and ghosts. Seeing the omens is my mother's affliction. Even the way she looks at herself in the mirror is filled with a struggle. I'm almost ashamed to admit it or think it, but I believe my mother sees someone else when she looks in that mirror. Someone else besides her. Something is always standing between my mother and her reflection.

News of the day. Hungary is being invaded—there are tanks in the streets and people are dying. The report is taking up most of the news. "Autumn Leaves" and Roger Williams. A Brylcreem commercial. A commercial for cigarettes with long filters making everything safe. The fishing report. The weather report. Time of the evening tide.

Sign of the cross. Push my uniform sleeves up to my elbows, and wash the drippings of capelin away from my hands and from under my nails. It's

October, and the view from the window over the sink is a cluster of mums and a row of purple asters. Most of the flowers have already died, or are preparing to hide beneath snow if they're the type to return in the spring, but asters and mums will survive until frost. My hands smell like they've been soaking in capelin for most of my life, and there's no way around it. Out the door, down the street. It's Bloomer Friday.

In addition to heavy brown stockings, a navy-blue uniform with its white collar and cuffs, and a gold cross on a chain at my neck, I'm wearing thick, navy-blue flannel bloomers. They extend from my waist to my knees. It's Friday, so there's physical education in the school auditorium.

We're learning English grammar, with rules about possessives, compounds, and conjugation, but there's already a feeling of doom and we wait to see who will be strapped. *Hold out that hand, young lady!* And we're down on our knees and up off our knees and wondering why in God's name—sweet Jesus and Mary—can't we ever get anything right? It's like something medieval—soldiers in armour—except in this case they're nuns, and they're all dressed in black, like outlaws in westerns.

And we're studying the minerals found in Newfoundland soil. Newfoundland is blessed with the most iron ore in the world—or very close to it—so we pray for the ore. Rocks right under our feet have been there for millions of years. The dinosaurs walked on the rocks—Newfoundland is that old. Their footprints are probably right in the centre of town if anyone bothered to look. Traces of dinosaurs walking down Main Street, looking for fresh leafy greens, not a cloud in the sky, not a care in the world. A clean salty breeze if they were close to a hamlet, trudging along at the end of the day, leaving their prints on every Newfoundland stone. Their footprints are probably on the rock in my room—a pink rock with pieces of mica. A rock older than Jesus himself and it's in my room on a shelf. That rock is older than Jesus and Pontius Pilate combined. Not a word of a lie if it's true.

The nun taps the bell on her desk and we walk single file to the school auditorium—silent, hands by our sides—and wait. A phonograph is perched at the edge of the stage and the nun drops the needle, cranks up the volume, and the entire class jolts forward, marching single file—in our bloomers—to the sound of "Be Kind to Your Web-Footed Friends." Some schools have soccer or tennis. We march along the four walls of the school auditorium, around and around, with our blue flannel bloomers, getting an incredible workout. I don't know why we have to wear bloomers in addition to the heavy blue uniform. Maybe in case we kick up a storm while we're marching in circles. No risk of underwear showing. We're silent marching soldiers for Christ, if girls are allowed to be soldiers. Otherwise we're soldiers' assistants.

Back to the classroom and a prayer for the day. Sign of the cross. Sound of the bell. Leave the building in an orderly fashion and out to the street. Down the hill, around the corner, up to Cobb Lane. Walk past the pond and the swans. Trees are a blaze of yellow and red.

People pick berries at the height of their season, and my mother picks leaves at the height of their colour. *Leaves past their prime won't hold their shade.* So every year, a bouquet of maple leaves, like flames soaked in shellac, glows on the brick and plank bookcase in a cream porcelain vase, silent and perfect. Never growing or moving. The bouquet could live with the nuns. Be right at home in a convent.

When I get to the house, my mother is taking the names of Jesus, Mary, and Joseph in vain while peeling potatoes and frying something or someone. The butcher knife handy. I open the door to the basement, take roller skates from a nail on the wall, go outside, attach the skates to the soles of my shoes, and roll down the sidewalk, a graceful skater sailing away, wind at my back—Barbara Ann Scott winning the gold for Canada at the Olympics. All the neighbours are cheering me on, waving me on. *You can do it, my luv. You can do it.* And after I've won the gold, they'll wave me into their yards with a big old-fashioned *Come on in* kind of wave. And we'll all have a cup of hot tea and something homemade. And they'll say *How are ye gettin' on, my luv?* And I'll say *Best kind!*

Then back to the house with my trophies and down to the basement. Dried leaves and flowers and bark. My own paste with water and Pillsbury flour. Everything balanced and glued to cardboard. Put a sheet of white paper over the flowers. Keep everything clean. Heavy books on top to keep everything flat. Pray, supper, pray. No one speaks at the table. My father makes the sign of the cross. I make the sign of the cross. *Gunsmoke.*

Up to my room and pray for Jesus to come back to the world. *Veni, Sancte Spiritus. Veni, Sancte Spiritus.*

End of the day and thoughts of tomorrow. The Saturday movie. *East of Eden. The King and I. Oklahoma.*

It's too cold to open the window. I can feel the chill right through the glass. The sky is filled with dramatic grey clouds, and even though it's only October, I can smell snow in the air. In a few weeks, all the men will be talking snow.

How are ye gettin' on, b'y? This weather would blow the horns right out of a bull.

The snow'll be fallin' so hard, b'y, ya won't see a hand before ya.

Pretty soon, b'y, it'll be snowin' by the reeves.

Yes, b'y, the evenin's are closin' in.

The glow from the street light spills over the yard and veranda, and a white moon is shining on rooftops and trees. Light of the moon on my face. Stars are pieces of diamond. I can see wind moving branches. Shadows falling all over the world.

During the day, my mother would see this as beautiful. Blue sky and rooftops and trees. Mums holding on in her garden. Sunlight all over town. But at night, there are only insurmountable fears. The whining of somebody's clothesline. Creaks in the hall. A tree scratching glass. She can't get the curtains pinned tightly enough.

My hands are still red from the strap, and they smell like capelin. I look directly into my own eyes in the glass, and the eyes look back and they want to be brave, like Katharine Hepburn.

Chapter Twelve

Speaking in a Foreign Language

It's 1957, 1958. Paul Anka and Ricky Nelson are on the radio. Pat Boone and "Love Letters in the Sand." "Wake Up Little Susie." The Asian flu is in China, Russia launches *Sputnik,* and Humphrey Bogart dies in Hollywood. *Father Knows Best. The Blob. The Fly. The Thing That Couldn't Die. Gunfight at the O.K. Corral. The Three Faces of Eve*—Joanne Woodward goes completely berserk because she's three people at once and loses her mind with a venetian blind in her hand. I will never forget *The Three Faces of Eve,* and I will never feel safe around a venetian blind for the rest of my life.

I don't understand why, or remember how it began, but I've started to speak with a foreign accent—something resembling French. But obviously not French, because I wouldn't know what I was talking about. And just after school and in shops where I don't know the clerks. When they ask if I'd like any help, I say *Ohhh, zank you. I vould like to find ze ribbon.* The clerk brings me to the right aisle and I say *Ohhh, zank you!* and pick out a package of rickrack or ribbon, walk to the cashier, and pretend to struggle with money as if I can't tell the Canadian dimes from the quarters. I'm pretending to be from away. That I'm not here for long. Just passing through.

It's after choir practice in the school auditorium. Whether we're able to sing or completely unable to carry a note, we take our places on the riser, shortest ones in the front. I'm centre front. We keep our eyes on the nun with a stick in her hand, then at the wave of her stick and stern look on her face, we move our lips like we're singing the Catholic heart right out of our bodies and pray to Almighty God that we get everything right. "Adeste Fideles." "Ave Maria." "When You Walk Through a Storm." *When you walk through a storm, hold your head up high, and don't be afraid of the dark.* If there ever were a song for my mother, this is the one.

It's mid-December and snowing. It's Newfoundland—it's always snowing. And it's coming down fast and the light is so bright that I have to squint to see where I'm going. The air is filled with everything cold and I dig my arms into my sides for warmth, a school bag with a mountain of knowledge tight on my shoulder.

There are two things I can't get enough of: movies and snow. Movies change anything that's going on in my mind, and snow changes the world around me. Snow transforming the town, icicles as tall as a house, and angel shapes in the snowbanks.

The funeral parlour, with its long white veranda, is almost invisible. Funeral parlours are like purgatory—a stop between our very last breath and whatever comes next. If you go straight from the graveyard to the hot fires of Satan, at least you get to enjoy a few days in the parlour. Unlike limbo, which is completely eternal, purgatory can last any number of years and then you're released—unless you have an indulgence saved up, which gets you immediately freed from your sin and sent straight to the arms of Jesus.

Cars are skidding, snow chains are biting into the ice, and sparks are flying. Shop windows are outlined with lights, snowflakes are sprayed on the inside of glass, and people are stomping their way from one store to another. *No matter what their religion, everyone's dollar is exactly the same.* That's what my father would say.

This is where my father's store should have been—before he lost everything and we had to move to the woods. It should have been next to the shoe store or the Lebanese jeweller. But my father's store was at the wrong end of town, between two taxi stands. People don't linger when they're getting a taxi. They leave as fast as humanly possible. The second problem was what existed on either side of the taxis: a saloon that was only open at night, and a garage.

When he still had the store, I'd walk there after Wednesday devotions—our extra thirty minutes of praying in church with the nuns, Kleenex pinned to our heads if we forgot a hat or a scarf—and I'd walk straight to his office and he'd be smiling as he saw me walking towards him. I felt so important to be walking into somebody's office with the large wooden desk and large wooden chairs, the tick of the wall clock, the phone and papers and folders and it all belonged to my father. But the store was in the wrong part of town and never had customers and we had to move to the woods. He just needed that store to be closer to people.

A woman is walking towards me and I slip on the ice and fall flat on my back. I've seen her before. She's always polished and poised and acts as if it took her no time at all to get dressed like a magazine model. She's wearing an olive-green coat with large matching buttons, brown leather gloves, a brown scarf, and a brown hat, and her olive-green purse matches her coat. I'm wearing a red and blue plaid winter jacket, a yellow and orange striped woollen cap, polka-dot mitts, and navy-blue snow pants pushed inside brown rubber boots. I recover my balance and a semblance of dignity, get up from the snowbank, and walk past her and through the centre of town. A walking, breathing booklet of paint chips.

Around the corner—watch the ice—and there it is spread out before me just like a painting: Cobb Lane covered in fast-falling snow. Birds are circling feeders and pieces of suet. The edges of houses are outlined with lights, and the colours are spilling across the yard like ribbons on snow. I stand at the edge of the road and look down at the frozen pond, which glitters like glass, snow swirling around me, and it's a painting as wide and as long as the sky. A tree in the foreground, laden with snow.

Pray, supper, pray. I speak, but it's never the right words to speak. The weather report. Christmas commercials. Johnny Mathis and Lawrence Welk. Alvin and the Chipmunks. Perry Como. Everything interrupted because of a possible storm—blowing snow, slippery and hazardous driving conditions.

My father listens with a serious look on his face. Should he drive the dangerous outport roads in the morning—one more trip before Christmas? Candy samples are packed in the trunk of the blue Chevrolet in front of the house. The house we're living in now is the fifth house we've lived in. We've moved, on average, every two years.

Upstairs and try to memorize everything—feel of the strap in my mind. Look out the window, bare feet on the cold canvas floor. Neighbours left their Christmas lights on and the red and green colours are melting into the snow. Sound of a car. My father snoring. Sound of my breath, sound of my heart, shadows on everything. Clouds are racing from one end of the black sky to the other. Moonlight is reflected on trees and my face is reflected in frost on the glass. Snowbanks are as high as the fence and higher. The two poplars are frozen like statues, their long black shadows falling across the yard, the snow, and the street. All trees are connected beneath the ground—that's my belief—and each time it rains, things grow closer together. The two poplars down by the gate may be connected straight down through the core of the earth to communist bamboo in China.

1959. It's the end of June and Queen Elizabeth leaves Buckingham Palace. She leaves England and comes to Canada. She comes to Newfoundland. She comes straight to our town, straight to Cobb Lane, and we watch her as she rides through the streets, and the skin on her face is like peaches and cream. Her face is like a porcelain doll's. Her skin is flawless. That's how close we are to her car. We can see the skin on her face and she waves to us as we're yelling and cheering and she seems just like a queen, which she is.

She has afternoon tea with important people in town in the beautiful Tudor inn. I've walked past the inn every day of my life—or close to it—so I can imagine what it must be like inside. I can imagine what it must be like to have tea with the queen, my fingers holding a bone china cup, gold at the rim and decorated with painted roses, and I'd say *Oh, thank you very much* when I'm offered an English cookie. And if my mother were there she could read the queen's leaves. But that could be a fatal mistake because my mother would get the penetrating look on her face and scare the bejesus right out of the queen and her assistants.

The queen had afternoon tea on Cobb Lane and it was all over the radio in Newfoundland and in the news all over the world and there were pictures in every paper, in every language. And for one full day, our town was totally famous, and beautiful Cobb Lane was in all the papers.

Newfoundland is in full, magnificent bloom again. Columbines, phlox, and pansies. Primroses, irises, and poppies. Flowers in hamlets and on the side of every Newfoundland mountain.

Downstairs, pray, breakfast, pray. Out the door. Down the street, up the hill, into school in an orderly fashion. Pray. Start of the day. The nuns strap us for any number of reasons, although they don't need a reason. Know the answer or don't know the answer. Strap, pray, end of the day. Sound of the bell.

A Christian Brother with a round, reddish face gives me a copy of *The Lives of the Saints.* A red hard-covered book—the colour of blood, symbol of martyrs.

He says, *Don't tell anyone that I gave you the book.*

He has his own office upstairs at the end of the hall and tells me to meet him at lunchtime one day a week. He's short for a man and stands exceedingly close and talks about saints. I don't know what to do with the book and I hate going into his room.

Cobb Lane is an explosion of colour and flowers. Roses and the smell of freshly cut grass. Sound of the birds. Two gliding swans. A sky so wide and with so many colours I'll never see everything. No matter what day or time I arrive, Cobb Lane is here. It's like meeting another part of myself.

Because I walk with my head bent most of the time, still have the tragic look on my face, and am generally quiet, people don't notice me. But I'm watching how others are living their lives—in stores, on TV, in Hollywood movies, at home. Edmund Hillary reaches the South Pole and

Elvis joins the army. Ice Pairs Championship won by Canada. Paul Anka becomes famous all over the world and he's a Canadian. People attend to their stores and their gardens and my father continues to pray.

Pray, supper, pray. Dry the dishes. The evening news. A report on scallops in Nova Scotia. Tuberculosis X-rays in Newfoundland. Charles de Gaulle. Time of the sunrise. Time of the morning tide. *The Honeymooners* and *I Love Lucy*. Homework, pyjamas, and I pray for a path that leads me directly to heaven or somewhere near heaven. I don't know if my mother secretly prays. If she does, she prays for control. The only person I've ever wondered about praying is Miss Mary Cobb. She must sometimes whisper a prayer in thanksgiving. Thanks for a small request granted. For being safe in a storm. For having the most beautiful fort on the face of the earth.

A breeze so light that it's almost unnoticed is filling the room. It covers my face and shoulders. Trees and flowers are resting. Stars are pieces of silver scattered on blue. Everything about this picture is gentle. But my mother can't see it. Or won't.

It's winter again and the world is covered with snow.

I dreamt I was walking alone on Cobb Lane and the swans turned into nuns and the nuns turned into a schooner and I sailed to Tangier. I was on deck with Gene Autry and Katharine Hepburn. It was windy and the wind threw spray on the deck but we sat calmly in deck chairs, just watching the water and birds, and the sea was silver in one direction and navy blue in the other. In Tangier, the market was filled with people selling canaries and flowers. There was a blazing hot sun and it was too bright for my eyes. There were crowds of people wearing veils, like the nuns, but I wasn't afraid. The houses were yellow and blue and the men were dressed in all shades of brown and the women were dressed in all shades of blue. Some people were eating cake and had cups of black coffee. Then it was dusk and the bells in Tangier were ringing and children were running around and stars were shining over the sea and the schooner. Then very dark night and a full yellow moon. Hundreds of people were standing around in a desert and I was there with Gene Autry and Katharine Hepburn. There was a king, and he told a wonderful story, which I can't remember, and everyone listened. Then he said, *May you always be blessed and protected.* Everyone, including myself, made the sign of the cross. Then I woke up. I'm even making the sign of the cross in my dreams. Anyone who happens to be in my dreams ends up praying.

Week after week there's news of Rwanda on the radio. Fidel Castro and Cuba. The St. Lawrence Seaway. Bobby Darin and "Mack the Knife." Hockey games are televised live. Jacques Plante is the only goalie wearing a mask, and some people call him a coward. *Have Gun—Will Travel. The Nun's Story* with Audrey Hepburn. All the nuns went to see that one. Two monkeys go into space and I'm in the kitchen with my feet on a chair, listening to the radio on Saturday night if there's quiet inside the house.

I'm writing short poems and a nun tells me I should talk to a priest.

Chapter Thirteen

1960

It's spring and Princess Margaret marries Antony Armstrong-Jones. *Ben-Hur, Psycho,* and *The Flintstones* on TV. The Cold War. Civil rights. Ireland and the IRA. Elvis is home after spending two years in the army, *Sputnik* re-enters the world, completely disintegrates, and we pray on our knees for the Communists.

I dreamt I was alone on a mountain. It was dusk, and the wind was perfumed with berries, pine trees, and earth. There was a hiking trail—partly maintained, partly neglected—and a highway hundreds of feet below. The trail was slippery from rain and I tripped on a fallen branch hidden in mud. Grabbed a tree near the ledge. Rocks tumbled over the cliff. Everything around me was spinning and I plunged to the highway, falling at an incredible speed.

I look through the window each morning, past the two poplars and the spinsters staring through their own glass. Thoughts of my mother, my father, my life at fifteen. My mother has to be going insane with her fear of the night and dark places. Fear of losing her mind. Of the unknown. Of losing control. Fear for her personal safety. The images she sees every day in the tea leaves. Sounds that swirl with the wind outside the house. Things that set her off every day. Sound of a clothesline at night. Fear of a tombstone, symbol of death. Fear of everything green. The penetrating look on her face.

My father's going in ten directions at once, prays part of the rosary morning and night, drums his fingers on the table sometimes, and continues to be strict with me.

I walk past our house in the evening, up a hill, to a view at the end of the street where I can walk right into the sky if I want to, and I want to take the picture with me wherever I go, keep it safe in my mind forever. A sky the colour of slow-changing blue. A setting sun and a rising sliver of moon. Sounds of the earth beneath my feet. Pine cones on rocks. Trees like enormous dark statues with long empty arms, or filled with an abundance of leaves in the summer.

The top of this hill is silent. No houses or buildings. No one walks by. Only trees on one side of the road and a graveyard on the other. The Catholic graveyard.

I still have my slightly pigeon-toed feet and a tragic look on my face, and I still don't know how to have a real conversation. It's all followed me for all fifteen years of my life. But it doesn't matter on the top of this hill, with its dark trees and sky, mountains folded around it like a body in sleep. The Beothuk walked here before me—there's no doubt in my mind about that. And they probably prayed in thanksgiving for the sacred view. Smoked from their long wooden pipes. Chanted in gratitude.

I look at the magnificent view—the majesty, vastness, simplicity. The freedom and power. The beauty of earth and sky. A sky as wide as the world. The peace and space. And there's only one thing I can think of to say: *thank you.*

Chapter Fourteen

Four Years After the Hamlet

Autumn, 1960. It's four years after Waltzing Matilda but it may as well be a thousand. Grade eleven, the last year of school, and discussions about the future. I can be a nun, a nurse, a wife, or a typist. *American Bandstand. What's My Line?* Vietnam. JFK wins the election. Time of the morning tide.

Newfoundland autumns are windy and brisk. Children fly kites and the colours soar above rooftops and steeples and mountains, above highways and forest and all the wild caribou. A kite lets you see the wind. Golden-red leaves are swirling to earth and my mother is preparing to shellac a display for the brick and plank bookcase, my father is arranging the blue Chevrolet for Christmas sales in the outports, and everyone is talking hockey.

That goalie is some shockin' good, b'y!

Ya got that right.

That stadium rink is freshwater ice, b'y. But ya know that yerself.

Yes b'y, that I do.

In my day, we played on freshwater ice and saltwater ice. Of course, saltwater ice made everything slower.

B'y is that ever the truth.

An exceptional hockey player moves to our town, a captain for a western Newfoundland team, and we can hear the play-by-play on the radio. He has a wife and a baby and they need a babysitter two nights a week and I'm hired. His wife's name is Jill, which reminds me of when we carried buckets of water across the Trans-Canada and down to the cabin. They appear to have a genuine interest in what's going on in my life, pay me ten dollars a week, and I save every cent—there's nothing I want to buy that's as important as saving.

They have magazines covering most of the top of a long hallway table. *Vogue, Life, Redbook,* and *Look.* "A Confidence Quiz." "A Personality Test." "Ten Ways to Increase Your Self-Confidence." "Five Steps to Complete Self-Esteem." I keep the information locked in my head, away from *Don't be so foolish.*

It's 1961. Day after day after day, news of Patrice Lumumba on the radio. The Congo and rebellions. Canadian troops are sent to help—they speak English and French and can talk to both sides, but it's hopeless. Assassination. Lumumba is dead. Yuri Gagarin becomes the first human being to go into space and orbits the earth. Elizabeth Taylor and *Butterfield 8*. "Are You Lonesome Tonight?" on the radio on Saturday evening. "It's Now or Never"—back-to-back Elvis. *Mister Ed*, the talking horse. News from the fishery: price of fresh cod—gutted, head-on. Messages for people in outlying regions.

It's three months before graduation and Jill wants to make me a dress. There are layers of white fabric and crinoline and lace on tables and armchairs. A thin white cummerbund. A strand of white pearls.

You need a lot of straight pins when you're making a dress. She's looking up from her living-room floor as she measures a hem. And I'm standing very still, inside a dress the colour of ice, with a basket of pins in my hand. I feel like a moth receiving a wing. I don't know why she's being so kind, but I'm grateful that hockey brought her into my life.

Jill's friend from away comes to visit and talks about the shades of white in the dress and how each shade of white has its own unique name, which I already know from the paint chips. She's an interior designer and I'm not sure what that means, but she's calm and composed and talks about texture, design, colour, and art. About drawing and painting. And lights begin to turn on in my brain. I want to be that. To study art and design. To be a somewhat-composed interior designer. And it all came together because of a game played on ice.

Every day, straight to the library's card catalogue *I* drawer. *Interior Design.* Bevelled glass. Gothic revival. Chippendale and *objets d'art.* Stairways and hallways. "What to Do with a Very Small Space."

I'm sixteen, almost seventeen. I dream about words I don't understand, clutch invisible objects and hold on for dear life, and in the morning my knuckles are sore. I finish my very last day with the nuns. The very last second. Sound of the bell. Sign of the cross. Up off my knees. Leave the building in an orderly fashion.

Graduation, diplomas, and a dance in the school auditorium. I'm wearing white pearls, small white earrings, white shoes with a slight heel, and one of the most exquisite white dresses ever created—a dress the colour of ice. And I'm grateful to every ancient Egyptian and Inner Mongolian. How did I get from the Inner Mongolians to wearing an exquisite white dress the colour of ice? Count it!

First, Egyptians invented a game played with sticks and a disk in 500 BC and centuries later the Inner Mongolians played the same game in a field. Then Nova Scotia, the 1800s, and the Mi'kmaq invented hockey on ice. And since the Mi'kmaq were related to the Beothuk, you might as well say that hockey was invented by the Beothuk right in the hamlet. The Toronto Maple Leafs can thank Shanawdithit. Then the hamlet bay turned solid with ice in the winter and children skated its white frozen surface for months, or raced down hills on pieces of old kitchen canvas, then home for warm bread and molasses. The Montreal Canadiens and Rocket Richard. The Hockey Hall of Fame. Then the exceptional hockey player moved to our town, Jill made me a dress, and here I am in the school auditorium in front of the Christian Brothers and nuns who watch every move, and we try to dance without actually dancing. I'm wearing an exquisite white dress, white earrings, and a strand of white pearls. Who knew I'd owe so much in my life to a game played on ice and invented by the Beothuk.

It's the middle of summer, a Saturday night, the baby's asleep, and a page in *Redbook* lights up like it's electromagnetic. "Schools for the Study of Interior Design." Montreal. Florida. Pittsburgh. I don't speak French—although there was a year when I spoke in a language resembling French. Plus, the French separatists in Montreal are blowing up phone booths. Florida's too far and I never learned how to swim. People in Florida are expected to swim. The Art Institute of Pittsburgh. All I know about Pittsburgh is the Pittsburgh Pirates, but I copy the number and start listing questions: How much will it cost? Where can I live? What do I need? How do I get from Newfoundland to Pittsburgh?

"Ramblin' Rose" and Nat King Cole. *Lawrence of Arabia.* Marilyn Monroe is found dead in her bedroom—one day she's in a Newfoundland airport, another day she's dead. The Cuban Missile Crisis.

I work and save for a year. Pack a suitcase and leave for the airport. My father hides in the airport restroom. I know he's crying. The blue Chevrolet in the airport parking lot—the glove compartment filled with organized paint chips, the trunk with candy and paint. My mother's rigid and solemn, the penetrating look on her face. Impossible to know what she's thinking.

I leave the town, the hamlets, and all the nuns. I leave *How are ye gettin' on, my luv?* Cross over the water and over a border. I leave the affliction behind, but I can see its face every time I look in a mirror. *And that's not a word of a lie.*

Chapter Fifteen

22 November 1963

It's early morning in the tiny room of a Pittsburgh rooming house. A single bed, a one-burner hot plate on top of a table, and a Westinghouse radio on top of a mini-fridge, which is on top of a bookcase. I'm nineteen years old, a student in art school, and the rest of the world is between me and the strap.

From my third-floor window I can see a White Tower Restaurant, a luncheonette, and a laundromat. Billboards. The roofs of neighbouring houses. A church on a hill, and streetcars inching their way through the streets. I can see the overhead wires and sparks shooting up from the tracks.

Everything's covered with a dusting of American snow. American people thinking American thoughts. Having American breakfast. And I try to imagine what it must be like to be an American. Pittsburgh is the first real city I've ever seen in my life, except for cities in movies.

Every Newfoundland sound is still in my head. The hamlet and lapping of waves, the salty spray on my face, the sound of crows and wind through the trees. Sounds of people weeding and hoeing and yelling from one yard to another. The nuns. My mother cursing. Sound of Newfoundland earth underfoot. Sounds on Cobb Lane. The Beothuk.

In an hour, Pittsburgh will be buried under a few inches of snow and the city will be at a complete standstill. In Newfoundland, people would trudge over the tracks, greeting each other as they struggled their way through the drifts.

B'y, ya can't see a hand in front of ya.

Drifts as wide as the devil's boots, b'y.

Yes b'y, but we'll do it in the long run.

That we will, b'y. That we will.

It's just after lunch in the art school classroom. A teacher walks into the room and says, *The president has just been shot!*

Someone yells back, *That's a terrible joke.*

He tells us it isn't a joke. *Pick up your books and leave.*

Everyone leaves the building and nobody speaks. A vacant look on everyone's face and a long ride home on a streetcar. Mothers holding their babies close to their breasts. Everyone silent. John F. Kennedy was assassinated while I was drawing a picture in Pittsburgh.

There's chaos everywhere on the face of the earth. News of the world from the small Westinghouse radio. The Pittsburgh Pirates and Vietnam in sometimes seemingly equal proportions. The Beatles and *Lord of the Flies*. Pollution, noise, and homelessness. The first diet drink: TaB. Elizabeth Taylor, John Diefenbaker, and Lyndon Johnson. Pope John XXIII dies, the first woman goes into space, and Buddhist monks are setting themselves on fire in the streets.

It's the end of the day in Pittsburgh. It's the end of the day on the entire North American continent. The sun has already faded, or is fading, right through the horizon. It's after supper everywhere. People on Cobb Lane have carried their laundry in from the line, although clotheslines are concealed on Cobb Lane—they're in backyards, behind fruit trees and arbours. Squeak of a pulley, turning of ropes.

The all-night laundromat that I can see from my window, with its fluorescent lights that are always turned on, is in darkness tonight. Not a single light showing. Every store and business in Pittsburgh is closed. Every store and business in North America is probably closed. The world has turned momentarily grey—all the colours drawn right out of it. The president was murdered as he waved to the crowds in Texas this morning.

The little laundromat boy that I see every weekend is probably home and asleep. He's eight or nine and watches a baby every Saturday morning. His father slumps in a plastic chair and reads from a book. The boy slumps in a chair like his father is slumped and reads a book with his eyebrows knitted, just like his father. He looks up when the baby whimpers, just as his father looks up. It's the same every week. He swaggers just like his father. Has an edge of anger just like his father. Everything about the child is adult. The only thing that indicates otherwise is the fact that he isn't. This little boy has never existed in a Newfoundland hamlet.

In a hamlet, for the most part, boys move through the ocean like fish in the summer and run on a wild, ragged beach. When the bay is frozen and frost eats away at the banks and trees struggle to hold on to the ground, they weave on sleighs around snowbanks and spruce with a wind so clean that if it happened to be a wall instead of the wind you'd be able to see right through it, as if it were made out of glass.

How did I get from the hamlet and my mother's affliction, from the leather straps and Cobb Lane and the tragic look on my face, to a Pittsburgh rooming-house window overlooking sparks from a streetcar at night? Count it!

First, something came into existence. Then somebody started to think and told a story. Somebody made a tool and everything changed. Then John Cabot discovered Newfoundland and the Beothuk. Railroads across the province. "Ode to Newfoundland"—*When sun rays crown thy pine clad hills.* The Great Depression, and it took years for Newfoundland to recover. I entered the world, someone tried to read the bumps on my head, and a few years later my father lost the store, our house, and all our possessions. Move to the woods. Back into town. Down on my knees, up off my knees. Praying ten times a day. Pat Boone and Patsy Cline. *The Twilight Zone.* Ed Sullivan on Sunday night. Westerns at the Majestic Theatre. Up to my room and looked out the window at night. Made pictures down in the basement. Found a place at the top of our road where I could walk right into the sky and beyond. Worked and saved every dime, and here I am in a rooming-house window at night, sparks from a streetcar, everything covered with a blanket of white. Wind kicking up layers of snow and sending them flying across wide, empty American streets. Sounds of pipes in the building, the jolt of a siren, a stranger's voice in the hall. The eyes of a girl reflected in the glass of a Pittsburgh rooming-house window at the end of November.

John F. Kennedy was shot and killed and Jacqueline Kennedy is tragic, stoic, and silent, as if she's completely made out of marble.

Chapter Sixteen

1964, Early Morning

There's a light summer mist—just enough to cool the city. The rooming-house window is open and a breeze is blowing its way through the curtains, through my hair, and into the room.

I take one last look at my view of Pittsburgh—the well-kept rooming-house lawn, the tops of sycamore trees, dozens of American people walking to American jobs, people waiting for streetcars. An American flag waves in a gusty American breeze. Rings of petunias circle trees on the sidewalk. School buses, taxis, and traffic. Pigeons fight over a thin crust of pizza. The red, green, and yellow of street lights. Grey factory smoke and a bridge in the distance. A skyline constructed from concrete and glass.

The Beatles appear on *The Ed Sullivan Show,* Queen Elizabeth visits Canada, and in Newfoundland the mortality rate of beavers is being discussed. *The Umbrellas of Cherbourg* and *Zorba the Greek. My Fair Lady.* Gomer Pyle. *Route 66.* A new Canadian flag is proposed, and the country enters a heated debate that will probably last most of the year. Frankie Valli and Vietnam. "The Times They Are A-Changin'." Agent Orange and Napalm.

I've learned to render the interior design of a doctor's waiting room, the design of a kitchen, design of a living room. *If you can't find the absolute perfect accessory, leave the wall bare!* That's the instruction. So I leave the wall bare and study ambient lighting, Art Deco, and the balance of colour. The columns of ancient Greece.

Morning news and the weather report: dampness and a chance of showers. There's always a chance of showers. They can happen anywhere without any warning. But it's still in the news.

Spiders come with the dampness and one is crawling over the window ledge and into the room. I brush it over the side and into the air because it's bad luck to kill it. When Joseph and Mary were fleeing to Egypt with Jesus, they came to a fork in the road. They chose a path, continued their journey, and a spider covered their path with a web. Herod's soldiers came to the fork, saw the web, figured no one could have gone that way, took the other road, and Jesus, Mary, and Joseph escaped.

By now the spider is down by the side of the house, its tiny head spinning from the impact of hitting the ground at full speed.

Lower the window, pick up the suitcase, out the door, down the stairs and the worn carpet runner, goodbye to the rooming-house people, return the key, and board a streetcar for the Greyhound bus to New York. A new home. Share the rent with a friend I met in art school. The window overlooks a small lawn with a chain-link fence and identical houses with identical lawns and metal fences.

It's 1966, and thousands of men in New York look exactly like Jesus—if Jesus happened to be in New York and waiting for a red light to change—right down to their bare feet and sandals and hair all the way down to their waists. Anti-war protests in Times Square and Grand Central Station. Canada doesn't enter the war and thousands of American men are crossing the Canadian border to avoid being drafted. The Hare Krishna are offering breakfast to anyone who wants a free bowl of oatmeal. Chant, wash your own bowl, out the door. Sitar music, Indian drums, and incense.

I'm working for a New York designer. Colour and fabric. Throw-pillow aesthetics—rectangular, circular, cylindrical, oblong, and bolsters. Silk, leather, cotton, or linen encasings. It's easy to feel overwhelmed with all the throw-pillow options, which is why people hire a designer.

The Mamas & the Papas come to New York. Janis Joplin comes to New York. Joan Baez, Judy Collins, and Buffy Sainte-Marie all come to New York. The Beach Boys, the Rolling Stones, and the Beatles come to New York. Bob Dylan lives in New York. Everyone eventually comes to New York. *Star Trek* and *Doctor Zhivago.* "Mellow Yellow." Ringo Starr and "Yellow Submarine." *In the town where I was born lived a man who sailed the sea.* It could be a song about any man who ever lived in the hamlet—it could be about Matilda's husband.

Civil rights. Women's rights. "Walk Like a Man." Miniskirts and heart transplants. A nude woman with a political message playing a cello—people tend to listen to naked musicians. Nuns don't have to wear their long black gowns anymore—no more veils hiding most of their face. No long wooden rosaries with a dangling Jesus tied to a loop on their belt. They wear skirts and blouses and stockings and we can see the shapes of their legs, and even though some of them look like actual women, I'll remember them otherwise every day of my life.

Sonny & Cher. "Masters of War." "The Ballad of the Green Berets." *We're on the eve of destruction* and I'm shopping for maroon-coloured candy, individually wrapped, to fill exquisite glass dishes, which match swatches of fabric and an exceedingly expensive maroon-coloured sofa in a New York furniture showroom. I shop for an hour and finally find them. I understand candy's importance. Saw my father sell candy for most of my life. Saw the brochures. Ate the samples.

In Newfoundland, my mother is reading her tea leaves or out in the garden, *Farmers' Almanac* opened to a phase of the moon. Time of the morning tide on the kitchen radio. My father is praying—he never stops praying. When he was a very young boy, he saw a Christmas concert in a school auditorium. An angel was suspended from an invisible harness. A hidden rope was silently pulled, and the angel slowly ascended up from the ground, up through the air, up past the top of the auditorium curtain, until it vanished. And as far as my father, the small boy, was concerned, the angel sailed directly to heaven. My father was sure he'd witnessed a miracle. And something about the miracle stayed with him. Even now, as a grown man—a salesman of candy, house paint, and cookies—he remembers the angel, and so he prays.

I've never stopped praying myself. Even on a revolving stool in a Chock full o'Nuts coffee shop, I'm giving silent thanks for date-nut bread with cream cheese. From the affliction, the nuns, and the hamlet, to Pittsburgh, the Hare Krishna, and Chock full o'Nuts, I'm praying at least six times a day.

Pittsburgh may be a typical American city, but New York in the sixties is unlike anything God ever intended. Unlike anything I've ever seen in my life, even in movies. Unlike anything anyone has ever seen in anyone's lifetime. A perpetual, pulsating, neon explosion. The homeless and crazy weave through traffic. Cars move without let-up, as if street lights are just one more neon display. Subway doors open and people spill from the train like gumballs, shoot across platforms, down flights of stairs, through tunnels, and up the stairs to daylight again. If New York happened to be a ball game instead of a city, it would be in permanent overtime. No home plate or bases. No uniforms. Just a pulsating Astroturf world with crazy people racing through stop signs and neon.

There are images of flag-draped caskets in every newspaper. Blood is seeping across the evening news. And despite everything going on in the world, I'm fully responsible for finding designer candy for a furniture showroom and organizing swatches of colour. I may be turning into my father.

I make anti-war signs, write anti-war poems, and read with desperate poets. March in protest in the middle of streets. There's fighting in every neighbourhood, not just in North and South Vietnam. I wear daisies and peace signs. Read letters my mother is sending about superstition and symbols. Read letters my father is sending—*Your mother is worrying all the time.* I attend meetings about swatches of fabric in furniture showrooms. There are eight sides to my brain.

I meet the most gentle and magical people I've ever met in my life at a small café theatre, and they outweigh every transgression I've ever encountered—they even transcend the affliction. Friendship, creativity, a safe place to be. Shirley Temple, Gene Autry, Christmas carols, opera. Underground, over ground, beyond description, and without restrictions. Twinkle lights, candles, cappuccinos, and trust. A pool of white light and a tiny stage opens up like a chakra. World of the Caffe Cino.

People clash with police, streets are combustible, and one night a stranger jumps out from the shadows and holds a knife right to my head, in the dark. I try to be calm and keep talking. I talk as if my life depends upon this conversation—which it does. But I fall anyway. I'm pushed—in the dark—at knifepoint.

From the hamlet and Waltzing Matilda to Cobb Lane, art school, and a knife in the dark in New York. How did I get to this moment? I try counting—because I can count anything. But it's the first time in my life that I'm unable to count. I don't know how I got to this moment.

I abandon the furniture showroom even though I spent years making sure fabric fit the mood of a room, and knowing what to do if a colour overwhelmed a small space. I abandon everything because my brain doesn't have enough room to count all the images swirling within it. This is like war, except now I'm the battleground.

Dominus, Dominus, Dominus vobiscum.

Evil may not be destroyable, but the saving grace is that neither is love.

1968. Warsaw troops invade Czechoslovakia and thousands of refugees are fleeing to Canada—everyone's fleeing to Canada. Protests are breaking out all over the world. "Jumpin' Jack Flash," Dr. Spock, "Hey Jude," and the Beatles. In New York, hundreds of anti-war protesters are beaten unconscious. Dozens of students are shot dead in Mexico City. Separatists riot in Montreal and *Apollo 8* orbits the moon. *The Carol Burnett Show* every week.

A fragile poet composes beautiful music and enters my life but is struck right through the heart by a heroin demon. We marry and hope things will change for the better. "Over the Rainbow," *Balm in Gilead,* "When You Wish Upon a Star," "Dream a Little Dream of Me." Odd jobs, bombings, and assassinations. Robert Kennedy. Martin Luther King. The streets are about to explode again and I'm about to become a mother. I get as far away as humanly possible. And on a clear winter morning, Newfoundland time—Newfoundland has its very own time zone—I give birth to the most beautiful child to ever inhabit the face of the earth and she is my daughter.

The hospital window overlooks snow-covered, glistening mountains. A town nestled beneath a blanket of fresh-fallen white. A *Pastel Blue* sky with *Silver White* clouds and a world of a thousand white paint chips. The new snow in gardens is so white and so fresh it's almost pale blue—*Icy Blue White.* Rooftops, under the glare of the sun, are *Pure White Enamel.* There's a golden sun and powdery moon in the same morning sky. The crisp winter air is as clean as a fast-running stream, and exactly six months later, two men fly right to the moon. I give birth to the world's most beautiful daughter and Armstrong and Aldrin leave earth and go straight to the moon. Johnny Cash, Bob Dylan, "Girl from the North Country."

From the straps, the nuns, and the affliction. From Cobb Lane, Pittsburgh, and war in the streets. From *Sesame Street,* Earth Day, and Woodstock, to the most beautiful child in the world and a man standing right on the moon. Half a million people chant *Peace!* in a field in upstate New York, but maybe they got it all wrong. Maybe half a million people were supposed to walk on the moon.

The sixties happened in a matter of minutes. I know, because I was the one counting it.

Chapter Seventeen

End of the Seventies, Autumn

It's the end of the seventies and I'm in the Catskill Mountains with their long, sweeping ranges of breathtaking scarlet and gold.

Every time I think I've had the strangest dream I'll ever have in my life, I have one that's even stranger. Last night I dreamt I was rehearsing a play in a restaurant owned by the nuns. I was Syrian, but people thought I was Italian and kept cursing the Arabs. I played a young mother, a waitress, who worked the night shift. In the play, I left the restaurant at midnight, and to save bus fare I walked across a vast frozen lake. It was stormy and windy and snow was blinding my vision. I walked towards a trap door in the stage—as I was supposed to. Stepped on imaginary thin ice and went through the trap door, screaming—as I was supposed to. The director and playwright were arguing over whether or not I should drown. They took a break, ordered lunch from the nuns, and I woke up—still under the floor and the ice.

There's a mild threat of rain and the window is open just enough to get a feeling of autumn. The white bedroom curtains brush against a piece of white quartz on the windowsill and a page begins to turn in a book, then stops, as if it's changing its mind.

It's almost two thousand years after Jesus. It's after the Vikings and it's after Shanawdithit, the final Beothuk—after her head went to England and was destroyed in the Second World War. News of the world in sixty seconds on everyone's radio. Kent State, Watergate, Nicaragua. "Rhinestone Cowboy." Captain & Tennille. The Vietnam War is over and done. Women in Switzerland are allowed to vote for the very first time and a total eclipse of the sun is witnessed in Newfoundland. From *Petticoat Junction* to Vietnam. From my mother's affliction to *All in the Family* and *Jaws.* Civil wars all over the world—in every paper, in every language.

I don't know what's on the Newfoundland radio, or what my mother is hearing as she's reading her leaves or heading out to the garden. She still has the affliction, but it's never discussed, or even acknowledged. Demons hide in every Newfoundland shadow. She dreams about knives crossed in a drawer, a curtain rod falling. She dreams about spiders. Of spilling the salt. Of everything green. My father still says the rosary every day of his life, and writes me short letters. *Your mother is always worrying. She's afraid all the time.* I don't know what my father is hearing or reading, but the news of the world is burning right through my table—ashes all over my feet. Elvis has been dead for over two years, but people are seeing him everywhere.

I'm living in a Catskill village with a touch of a Newfoundland hamlet. Forest and stillness without any trace of an ocean, but there's a mighty reservoir just a few miles away—122 billion gallons of drinking water for all of Manhattan. Because all things in this world are basically linked, when I'm walking along the edge of the reservoir, which flows under the Hudson, which flows into the Atlantic, which is the same water surrounding the Newfoundland hamlet, I'm practically strolling with Waltzing Matilda.

The reservoir spreads before me like a map of the world, if the world happened to be covered with a large piece of blue silk. It's a massive body of *Ink Blue* water, silent and smooth as glass, everything surrounded by mountains and forest. Everything framed with branches. The reservoir water is reflecting the trees, and branches sway like a trapeze in the circus.

The circus came to our town for a week every summer. The carousel, Ferris wheel, and guess-your-weight games. Break a row of balloons with a dart. Cotton candy and smell of hot buttered popcorn. The acrobat people. A dwarf. The woman on a flying trapeze. Oh God, that's who I wanted to be. Moving in space, above the tops of the trees. That would be me—sailing across the Newfoundland forest, barely touching a leaf. I loved all the mystery and magic. A stagehand would pull a switch or a rope and a miracle would happen right in front of me. And I'd watch every move. I'd never believe it if I hadn't seen it with my own eyes. And we'd all say, *Can you believe it? Can you ever believe it?*

The trapeze woman would cling to the bar as if she were clinging to life, which she probably was, then release her entire body, sail through the air like a bird, and be caught by someone on another trapeze with his arms reaching towards her. How could she trust someone that much—trust that someone would be in the right spot, up in the air, at the very right second? If I ever did that with a nun, I'd die on the very first leap. The nun would vanish and I'd plunge right to the ground. The nun would have moved the net to teach me a lesson. *Prayer would have saved her, if she'd prayed often enough.* That's what they'd say after I'd plunged to my death.

When the trapeze act was over, I'd watch the magnificent carousel horses—their wooden legs moving through space, their wooden manes streaming behind as they ran right into the wind and carousel songs filled the air. "Meet Me in St. Louis, Louis." "The Sidewalks of New York." "In the Good Old Summer Time." And I'd pick my favourite horse and buy tickets for multiple rides every summer. I can see that circus and the flying trapeze in my mind whenever I want to.

I watch the swaying reflections, then sail up from the darkness, clutch a flying trapeze, find my balance in less than a second, and sail over the Catskills, right through the top of the world's largest blue tent and up to exquisite white mountains hidden in clouds. Somewhere like that. And for as long as I'm on that trapeze in my mind, and for as long as I can maintain my balance, I can sail above mountains and forest and into the stillness and just about anywhere.

No matter where stillness happens to be—no matter which mountain or forest—it's exactly the same. Whisper of wind. Water and sky. Sound of a bird. Stillness is in the rocks and shadows of Stonehenge. On a hamlet beach in the evening—a flaming sun and a few gulls calling an end to the day. It's in an isolated shrine in Kyoto, Japan—incense and somebody praying. It's a place to prepare for whatever comes next. Stillness is the same in Polish and French.

If I give my mind the freedom to wander as far as it wants to travel, it may never return. Would embark on a journey that could take forever to finish, and I'd be standing right here, next to 122 billion gallons of water, unable to think because I'd been deprived of my mind.

The sun is melting into the Catskills again, the air is crisp with the smell of autumn and spruce trees, and with every step, my feet sink into layers of leaves, pine cones, and moss.

I leave the trapeze soaring above reservoir water, but I keep the carousel music safe in my mind. Back to the village minus an ocean. To the kitchen and a cup of Earl Grey.

There are pieces of paper in every corner of my apartment, and if people rushed through the door in need of a place to sit, they'd all have to stand. Scraps of collage work. Bottles of glue. Stacks of writing. There are no more journals because I don't want to know what I'm thinking every day of my life.

The only clear space is the kitchen table, and if you're from Newfoundland, which I am, you can get used to living much of your life in a kitchen. It's sometimes the only room in a house with anything resembling heat. In the hamlet, a kitchen is the place for a Saturday party—everyone gathered around a warm pot-bellied stove. Sounds of an accordion and fiddle. Singing, step-dancing, and folk songs—"I'se the B'y" and "Squid Jiggin' Ground." And between the singing and stomping and dancing, they'll have a sandwich in one hand, a drink in the other, and a thick slice of partridgeberry pie within reach because there isn't a third hand to hold it. The parlour is for funerals and Christmas.

In addition to paper in every corner of the apartment, tonight there are bundles of snapshots. They usually live on an overhead shelf in boxes covered in something resembling velvet. But because it's good to let them breathe every once in a while, tonight they're in small, organized stacks—like playing cards in a Las Vegas casino, if Vegas happened to be in the kitchen instead of Nevada. Everyone pictured is now ten, twenty, forty years older.

A scholar's ink lasts longer than a martyr's blood. That's what Matilda or my uncle would say. The same can be said about film in a camera. It all comes down to the photographs—like code words, revealing a person or place.

Birthday parties on a rocky Newfoundland beach—the 1950s, and large woollen blankets. Kool-Aid, sandwiches, sandflies, and the coldness of calamine lotion. Sound of the waves heard in a shell. A picture of a First Holy Communion—tiny fingers clutching a rosary, the eyes filled with something like the silence of smoke. Children in school with the nuns and lined up in front of the bishop. Down on our innocent knees, in front of his legs, kissing his ring. That was the rule.

Two children inside an alpine chalet—girl on the left, boy on the right—my mother's weather barometer. The girl comes out when it's sunny, the boy comes out when it's raining, and each wears appropriate clothing. The barometer lives with the plants so they'll know what to expect.

Large glossy photos of a café theatre in New York in the sixties—everyone surrounded by friendship, candles, and trust. A snapshot at the top of the Empire State Building at night, and the wind is blowing so hard that if I don't grasp a rail, I'll be blown over the side. A picture of two once-beautiful people—a marriage that just wouldn't work. Two beautiful pieces and you want them to fit, and you move them around, but one starts to break and nothing is gained when somebody breaks. Single parenthood—make every single end meet. Try to be just like my father, exactly. Do ten things at once. Drum my fingers on top of a table sometimes.

Children in raincoats in upstate New York. Raccoons on a porch. Cardinals on a windowsill, waiting for food. A night sky as seen from a spaceship—the light from 10 million homes. Ten times 10 million. A grid of glowing humanity.

A photo of a man looking down at his watch. A circle of people discussing touches with madness. It was the tenth anniversary, right to the minute, of his only son's suicide.

People speak in turns about families in danger, about war in their country. In war, flesh is pulled away from the face like skin from an onion. The mystery of suffering. An image of pain and it won't fit in the box neatly. It bleeds over the edges. People speak about symbols they cherish. A scapular. A small stone. A photograph—everyone in the world has a photograph.

A picture of sudden light on a building. A warm, golden-pink twilight that appears without warning and won't last forever. A hawk, black as pitch, soars through the sky, and it's lit from behind with that golden-pink glow, and for one instant it's a view of magnificence.

A snapshot of a small Newfoundland hamlet at night with stars in the millions. Sounds of a bay. Lobster pots, beaches, and forest. Silence except for wind racing through trees. Lapping of waves on the shore. Where everyone has a cup of hot tea and something homemade at the end of a day. Where everyone knows everyone's name.

A snapshot of New York and a skyline like diamonds that have wrapped themselves around the throat of a city. A full silver moon in a starless black sky. The sound of crazy people racing through traffic. Thousands of anonymous voices, anonymous music from anonymous buildings. Where no one knows everyone's name. It's just like the hamlet, only opposite.

I finish the cup of Earl Grey and take a quick look at a weekly paper. News of yard sales and yoga. A school concert. Children singing. I've never forgotten the little girls from those early years. Never forgotten the classrooms or forgotten the word *'ope.*

There are long, thin clouds above the Catskill Mountains tonight, and a sliver of moon, and even though the windows are closed, winter is creeping across the mountains and into the room.

I look at my eyes in the glass and a thousand people look back. I've stopped worrying about God—whatever it is, whatever its name. I've stopped wondering. I've figured it out.

Chapter Eighteen

Central Park, Start of the Eighties

It's evening and it's snowing in Central Park—a soft, steady snow, like feathers spinning their way down to earth. The Empire State Building is in three shades of blue and the skyline is shimmering with 3 million glass windows. A soft breath of wind and everything viewed through a scrim of falling white snow. It's been forty years since I first started out in the world, right to the minute, and I'm living in downtown New York.

It's the start of the eighties and my dreams have become one rushing scene after another and they go by so quickly I can't remember what they just were—just that I dreamt them. It's after two different countries, eight different towns, and nineteen different homes. Different birds flew past different windows.

Pierre Trudeau takes a long walk in the Canadian snow and retires. Pope John Paul II leaves the Vatican, crosses the ocean in a jumbo jet—unlike Jesus, who would have probably walked—goes straight to a Newfoundland hamlet, and talks to the fishermen. It's the two hundredth anniversary of Newfoundland's first Catholic church. The pope goes straight to the fishermen because that's the first thing people think of with Newfoundland—the fish. From Christopher Columbus to Pope John Paul II, it's always been fish. He blesses the boats, and Matilda may have mentioned the factory boats lit up like a city out in the ocean, dragging the water, and how they stole the livelihood from thousands of Newfoundland families. The pope blesses the fleets and the children and teachers, meets with the handicapped, returns to the Vatican, and Michael Jackson's hair catches on fire during a Pepsi commercial.

If it's snowing in Central Park, it's snowing in Newfoundland—it's always snowing in Newfoundland. The Manhattan skyline is covered with the spectrum of twilight, from violet and blue to gold. Twilight covers the rivers. It covers the Hudson, a river originating so far north that it's almost in Canada. The Hudson flows from a lake in northern New York down to the mouth of the Atlantic Ocean and Lower Manhattan, and the very same ocean surrounds every Newfoundland hamlet. So whenever I walked on the shore in the hamlet, I was actually in part of New York.

If you're ever lost in the woods, follow a river downstream. Someone always lives at the end of a river. That was my mother's advice. So if I got lost in the Newfoundland woods, I could follow a river, and someone would find me in downtown New York.

Central Park is silent this evening except for the soft crunching of boots. An elderly man with a violin sits alone on a snow-covered bench. The bare trees behind him are covered in white like a long row of ghosts. He's playing "Oh Holy Night" and snow is falling around him and the skyline is glittering like 10 million diamonds and I've walked right into the middle of somebody's dream except in this case it's real. And I stand off to the side, just slightly inside the picture.

I'm inside the world's largest snow globe and someone just turned a key and "Oh Holy Night" is filling the air and I'm moving in a very slow circle around the base of Manhattan with snow falling around me like feathers, the stars brightly shining, and the old man looks up and he says, *How are ye gettin' on, my luv?*

And I say *Best kind,* because how can I not be? I'm inside my very own snow globe. With my very own song. My very own key.

Chapter Nineteen

Manhattan, a Morning in June

End of the eighties. A New York apartment. New York windows are always a gamble. In the morning, the very first view can be of a brick wall. Or traffic flowing like a honking red river. Or a sky crowded with layers of clouds—if a sky could ever be crowded, it would be in New York. Or it can be a clear view of anonymous lives, so close you can see what they have on their shelves—can almost tell what they're thinking.

Completely by chance, my view is of a small private courtyard with benches and flowers, a manicured hedge, and a Rousseau-like tree as tall and wide as a house. A high wire fence separates the courtyard from the rest of us in the neighbourhood. My view is no longer the hamlet and bay. And it hasn't been the Catskills for years. It's an old magnificent tree.

In summer the tree is alive with sparrows, cardinals, and an occasional squirrel. In autumn it blazes like topaz. Winter snow rests on branches like hankies. It's been a trusted, reliable friend at the end of the day.

When it's early enough and quiet enough, before trucks and construction and sirens, and there's a soft, warm breeze like there is now, I look past the tree, past chimneys and rooftops, and into the clouds, and I can imagine the view from the top of that Newfoundland hill where I could walk right through the sky and beyond.

My music drifts through the window and out to the branches. Mozart, flute music, John Fahey's guitar. I've stopped listening to music with words. I've heard enough views and opinions.

The Berlin Wall has completely crumbled and Archie Bunker, Hawkeye, and Maude are over and gone. A high-school graduation, a daughter in a blue cap and flowing blue gown, and enough cherished memories to last for a lifetime. *The Waltons* has been cancelled for years, but I'll remember the names forever. *Good night Grandpa, Good night John Boy, Good night Mary Ellen.* Wayne Gretzky is named the best NHL player since the beginning of time and he's a Canadian, and for one shining moment all is right with the world. Joey Smallwood is dead and the world is consumed with AIDS. Rock Hudson and Liberace both died from AIDS. Thousands have died and thousands are dying. I've lost twenty-three friends and they can't be replaced.

Hospital rooms smell like bleach. Entire bleach-smelling wards. I try not to be like my mother. I try to hold the skeletons propped up in bleach-smelling beds—skeletons wearing t-shirts three sizes too large. Chat with a friend as he empties his stomach through a small plastic tube. Gay plague. Epidemic. Exhaustion. Dementia. Kaposi's sarcoma. Fear and the terrible weight of pain. Glaring hospital lights replace the warm glow of living-room candles. The small café theatre from the sixties is dying before me. It isn't just my friends that I'm losing. I'm losing myself.

I empty apartments and that's a pain all of its own. What to save from a life can be easy. What to get rid of is easy. It's the thousands of things in between—that's the problem. Icons and photos and items from childhood saved for a lifetime. A single dried rose in an ornate gold frame. What did it mean? A collection of music—proof that they'd been on this earth. A collection of glass and porcelain pigs. What do you do with two hundred porcelain pigs from various spots on the globe when they're carefully catalogued—each one with a name—and they're in alphabetical order and they're all looking you right in the eye? What do you do with two hundred glass pigs with names?

The Beach Boys and acid rain. The Gulf War and Rwanda. Free Trade Agreement. Dalai Lama. *Cheers* and *Murphy Brown*. Princess Diana and Mother Teresa.

My father continues to pray night and day, but my mother has turned into a truck—an out-of-control, broken-brakes, driving-in-the-night-without-lights kind of truck, running over everything that happens to be in her path. Whatever once filled her with irrational fear has now filled her with irrational rage. Almost a vengeance. She's swollen with anger, with food, and with fear. The only thing different is that we've all gotten older.

Fast Newfoundland visits and the smell of a wild, salty ocean, a bold ragged coastline. Let Newfoundland earth fall through my fingers. Watch fog lifting itself from the bay. My uncle is telling a yarn to anyone who will listen. *Now, did you ever hear a story like this one?* Sign of the cross, end of his day. Matilda's husband, the man who could knit a bicycle from a ball of steel wool, has passed away. Gone to the great hereafter. A long day of fishing, then dead. *'E wouldn't 'ave wanted it any other way, my luv. The church service was out of this world. I didn't know we 'ad so many friends.*

Chapter Twenty

Y2K

Computers may crash all over the world, and I'm in a Manhattan library waiting to use a computer and risking complete self-explosion. A man is sitting in front of my terminal and his right hand covers his face. I touch his arm and he jumps. He's a homeless middle-aged man asleep at terminal one, and he apologizes for taking the chair. For having so many bags. His body is filled with shame. Guilt is *I made a mistake.* Shame is *I am a mistake.* He disappears through the library door and out to the street, past rushing pedestrians, until he's invisible.

My nosebleeds have stopped, but the dizziness hasn't. It knocks me right to the ground sometimes. Knocks me unconscious. I read that some people, because of upbringing and life situations, are more likely to survive in this world. If that's true, I'll live forever.

It's a few hours before the stroke of the millennium at Harbourfront, Toronto and thousands of people are waiting to see if the world will come to an end after the fireworks display.

It's February 2000 in New York City and earth continues to spin. Fifty-six years have all slipped away since I entered this world and God alone knows how it happened because it escaped me. The years are whizzing by like bullets but I still try to count them.

Someone discovered the earth, somebody threw a rock, and war was invented. The Crusades. Henry the VII gave John Cabot money to purchase a ship. Cabot crossed the ocean, found Newfoundland and the fish, planted a flag for Great Britain, and settlers destroyed every Beothuk. The First World War and 9 million people were killed. Electricity and sliced bread. Christmas trees with bubble lights in the living room. "When the Moon Comes Over the Mountain." Humphrey Bogart, the Second World War, and 60 million people were killed. The nuns and down on my knees and something in Latin. The Korean War and Princess Elizabeth became the queen. The sixties, Vietnam, and test-tube babies. Transcendental Meditation. Jet planes around the globe and I fly from New York to Toronto in a matter of minutes and here I am standing alone in a hospital doorway in Toronto.

My mother is old and alone, an IV attached to her arm. She's eighty-three years of age. Two small stuffed animals are asleep on her chest and they move up and down as she takes long, heaving breaths. She looks like a large, frightened child, alone in room 666 in the sterile ward of a Toronto hospital. If a hospital ever had a room with that number, and in this case it does, my mother would be the one to receive it.

There are tubes of lipstick in a bowl on the bureau, a bottle of Tweed perfume, flowers from someone, get-well cards, and a bottle of pills with a handwritten note of directions. And I'm slightly afraid of her even though she's almost unconscious. Still afraid that the affliction will come roaring up from the bedsheets without any warning and go screeching around the room. All the old memories are still in my brain—time didn't change anything.

She doesn't remember me, but I tell her my name, and I have no way of knowing if she knows who I am or understands what she's seeing. I could be a leaf inside one of her teacups. I could be a symbol of doom. I open the box of miniature peppermint patties that I picked up on the way, and put one in her hand. She lifts it close to her face, then her arm drops to the bed—it's too heavy.

Her head is deep in the pillow and her body is motionless. Only her eyes are alive, and they're hallways—passages. I wander the hallways of her eyes, through all the places I've lived as a child, as a young girl, and as a woman who became a mother myself. I see her face everywhere. Her handprint is stamped on my sky, on every attribute of my being.

In an almost inaudible voice, she whispers that Pat is out in the hallway. *Pat is in the hall every day.* And I listen for more, but that's all she says.

Pat was her younger sister and died from cancer. Pat never cared that my mother married a Lebanese Catholic, and my mother didn't care that Pat married an American serviceman and lived most of her life on an American base. It all became some sort of bond. If there's any help crossing over to the great hereafter—if there is a hereafter—Pat is the perfect person to help.

My mother whispers that people are trying to crawl through the window, and I tell her she's on the sixth floor, it's impossible. But I look through the window for a very long time to assure her that whoever was out there is gone.

The hospital table is pushed to the foot of her bed and is empty except for a cup. Probably for a cup of warm tea, except she can barely breathe, let alone swallow.

The cup is white with three black dots in a vertical row. One, two, three. Faith, hope, and charity. Or three of the seasons: winter, summer, and fall. You can have a Newfoundland year without spring—just go from a long, hard winter straight into summer—but you can't have a year without fall. Or three summer months: June, July, and August.

A summer of Sundays. 1949 or 1950. Kindergarten or grade one. It's before we lived in the woods—an earlier house. I'm young. Five or six.

My mother's father loves to go for a Sunday drive. He loves the clean country air. So every Sunday we go up the highway to the home of a relative. I'm on the front seat between the two men. My mother is in the back with the affliction. Our car reaches the place on the highway where the relatives live. There's a pasture with a cow wandering an expanse of green.

Be a good girl and keep your grandfather company, and my parents leave the car, walk through the field, out of sight, and down to the house for a visit.

My grandfather remains in the car. I remain in the car. My grandfather's leg is bad every Sunday and he can't make the long walk through the field and down to the house. My grandfather removes his glass eye, props it up on the dashboard, above the radio, which is turned off, and he says to be quiet.

I'm five or six and do what I'm told and he leans over, both hands up under my dress, pulls down my panties, large hands right up inside me, and he moves closer. And he doesn't look at me. He looks straight ahead, as if I'm not there. I look straight ahead. Up past the glass eye on the dashboard and through the dusty car window. I can hear cars whizzing by and I start to feel very small.

Be a good girl.

I pray for people who never come up from the big house. I pray to be a cow in the pasture. I stay in the car in an orderly fashion. Thoughts of the strap and something in Latin and down on my knees. *Dominus, Dominus, Dominus vobiscum.* I pray and I'm quiet. Clouds of dust fall on the windows like curtains.

I pray that someone will come up from the house to see if I want a glass of cold water. The water is in a grey metal bucket inside the front porch by the door. They just have a well. There's a round wooden cover on top of the bucket and a blue and white ladle with small specks of white on very dark blue. *Holy Mary, Mother of God.*

❖

I've tried to get away, in my mind, from the little girl on the front seat of that car—abandoned, aching, the old man next to her. But her large, haunting eyes will forever stare back through a dusty car windshield. Specks of gravel and dirt from the road.

Men who sexually abuse their granddaughters often sexually abused their own daughters when they were children—that's the belief. If that's true in my own case, then my mother is almost unforgivable.

Maybe a pope could forgive. Or he might just throw up on his red satin shoes if he knew the whole story. Maybe Jesus himself, if he happened to be standing outside on the highway, his white robes covered with dust, could forgive. But try as hard as I might, I can only get to *almost forgive.* It's in the far distant past, the present, and future. It's inside me. The mind forgets nothing. Even the skin remembers its life.

We've never discussed this and it isn't possible now. What was left unsaid will be silent forever.

I don't know why the hospital cup is right there on the table, all by itself, within easy reach. Maybe for water. I soak a small piece of sponge and hold it close to her lips. Let a few drops find their way into her mouth and roll down her throat.

I make her one last Valentine heart from the foil wrapping inside the box of peppermint patties and hold it high in the air. She's unable to speak but she sees it and her eyes fill with tears. I hold her paralyzed hands and think of our past, but it's far too much to remember.

It's night. She's unable to swallow, no medications are being administered, and she's being left to die on her own.

My father sits on a hospital chair in the only shadowed part of the room. Except for a few hours of sleep during the day, he's stayed beside her for weeks. *Till death do us part*—and he won't leave until then.

Her chest heaves with slow, wheezing gasps, and the nurse says, *If you touch her hand and call her name, she may open her eyes, but she's exhausted.*

I say *Hi Mom. Can you say "Hi"?* I say it over and over. And I say a silent Hail Mary because praying is the only thing I can think of.

She opens her eyes and says, almost inaudibly, *Hhhhhhiiiiiiiiii*—as if now that she's started the word, she's completely incapable of ending it. As if she's exhaling the end of her life. *Hi* is her very last word.

After a silence, we speak of days filled with mercy. Memories that made it all bearable. A few days when she was happy.

I kiss her forehead and her skin is like ice. As if she'd been out on a pond, skating for hours and braving the furious Newfoundland elements.

My father reaches for the chain on a wall light shining directly above her. Its harsh glare makes her pale skin appear even whiter—*Bone White, Icy Blue.* His clothes are wrinkled, and his eyes, which I can finally see, are swollen from tears. He would normally ask permission to turn off a hospital light, but he's not asking tonight. He's closing his own private story. The parable of the Lebanese Catholic man and his Scottish Presbyterian wife. Except for light from the hallway, the room is plunged into darkness. The walls and the ceiling are black. The bed is black. A black floor. The windows are black. Nothing but night surrounds her. There is only darkness and the stone cold face of my mother, like a head carved from white marble. A look on her face defying description. Almost rage—if rage can be a final emotion. She's come face to face with the night and whatever she feared—and on her own terms, when she was dead. In the hereafter.

No one tells us when it's appropriate to walk away from the dead. It's a quiet, personal decision. My mother's body looks like petrified wood.

There's silence in room 666 and all the way down to the hospital lobby. It's the middle of night. It's night over the entire North American continent. Silence out on the street. It's black as pitch and Toronto is covered with a thick layer of snow. Trees and buildings are black. Cars parked on the side of the road are black. The sky is a large black sheet. It's blacker than ink. A splatter of silver stars. Not even a cloud. Not a breath of wind. It's as if the entire universe is reinventing itself—starting over from the very beginning of time. Someone discovered the earth and somebody threw a rock and the other person tried to forgive because it couldn't go on forever. Earth was covered with trees and birds. Lap of the oceans. Somebody learned how to sing and taught the others. "Ave Maria," "The Old Rugged Cross," "Santa Lucia," and all the rest. And since Newfoundland was discovered by then, everyone had their own mug for a cup of hot tea and something homemade.

Chapter Twenty-one

Final Prayer

In the morning there's snow all over Toronto and I'm trudging through drifts, in some places up to my knees, looking for pansies because that was her favourite flower. No one has pansies in the middle of winter and it's snowing to beat the band. Snowing like there's no tomorrow. The florists are useless. I'm crazy for asking. Then, like a neon mirage above a mountain of snowbanks, Walmart rises before me. Tim Hortons, McDonald's, Canadian Tire. A shopping mall bursting with clothing, housewares, fast food, and makeup. Snow tires and tools. I'm looking for something I don't anticipate finding, but I'm holding on to the goal. *Zellers!*

Do you have a gardening section?

The clerk looks bewildered. It's snowing so hard that we can't see the street.

I don't know. Did you try the basement? She answers me with her own question as John Denver sings about jet planes and airports. No one is leaving the Toronto airport today.

Down the escalator to a dimly lit corner with work gloves, flowerpots, and Miracle-Gro. Plastic flamingos and elves holding lamps. My eyes scan the walls. Plastic roses. Grapevines in the shape of a wreath. Plastic ferns. Plastic sweet peas for a trellis in spring. Garlands of tiny silk pansies. Hundreds and hundreds of pansies. Thousands of pansies. Blues and violets, yellows, vermilions, reds.

Up the escalator, straight to the checkout, out to the unshovelled sidewalk with shopping bags overflowing with blooms. A bus to my father's apartment. Five hours later, a three-foot Styrofoam wreath is complete, and the wide-eyed faces of two hundred pansies in every colour Zellers had on display look up in amazement. My father sits in his chair in silence. No TV, radio, or conversation. There's barely a light. His mind is elsewhere. Or blank.

In the morning, the sky is clear, the air is frigid, and I head for the funeral home with two hundred pansies. All funeral parlours are exactly the same. Serious people in dark, impeccable clothing stand near the door and there's an overwhelming feeling of death. Heavy draperies in non-threatening colours—*Soft Topaz, Light Ivory, Sky Blue, Beige.* Beautiful but uninviting and uncomfortable furniture. End tables with lamps and boxes of tissue. Flowers on dark, polished sideboards. Scrubbed polished floors. Everything's under control. There's no need to worry. Faint smell of roses. Someone whispering *They're holding up well.* A book for signing—solid proof that you're not the one in the coffin. A table with sympathy cards.

I walk to the coffin and I don't know if she knows that she's dead. The cover is closed—for two days it was open. I lean the Styrofoam wreath with its two hundred pansies against the gleaming brown wood, and I don't know if the affliction is dead or hovering somewhere, but I leave the wreath with its large red pansy *E* in the centre and return to my pew. Red was her favourite colour. Pansy was her favourite flower. Her name was Elizabeth.

"Nearer, My God, to Thee." "Be Not Afraid." *The Lord is my shepherd; I shall not want. He maketh me to lie down in green pastures: He leadeth me beside the still waters. He restoreth my soul.* And her life is completely over, just like that, with a prayer.

A week later I return to New York in the middle of the night and carry my bag and my mother's ashes up four flights of stairs, put water on for a cup of hot tea, walk to the window, and look through the glass to a complete and terrible emptiness. The entire tree is gone. A freshly sawed-off stump stands in its place. I yell *Why!* even though it's the middle of the night and there's no one to ask, and I stand at the window and stare through the glass and I can't stop staring because if I wait long enough and stare long enough the tree may appear.

In the morning, the man who looks after the courtyard is checking a flower bed.

Can you hear me! I scream.

He looks up at the fourth-floor window. *Yes?* He's anticipating a question.

Why was the tree chopped down! I'm screaming and in a state I can't name—a state I don't recognize.

Because six weeks out of every summer, it drops things and no one can sit here.

I have a clear view of cement and brick walls. A house with four windows. Eight panes of glass in each one. Thirty-two. Three and two. Five.

A bird flies towards the now-vanished tree, then lands on a hedge.

My father never moved to the centre of their large double bed. He sleeps on the side he inhabited for almost six decades, as if his wife is still resting beside him. Needing him. He holds her safe in his mind, and will continue to hold her for the rest of his natural life. Whatever God grants him.

Chapter Twenty-two

After Everything That Ever Happened

It's been seventy years since I first started out in the world. It's hundreds of years after the Beothuk. Decades after the hamlet—although, to this very day, I can hear it and see it and smell the salty Atlantic. It's after so many people were born and so many died.

It's raining long, thin ribbons of rain, and the ribbons are falling against a backdrop of moonlight. It's snowing and the flakes are like feathers. Sunlight is bursting through open windows and the breeze is a perpetual whiff of sweet roses. It's stormy and the wind is vicious and angry and people are running for cover. It's rare Newfoundland flowers and rocks that are 400 million years old. It's the flashing of neon, the silence of snow. Sounds of the wind. Faces in windows. Traffic or no traffic. It's a friend at the end of a day.

It's a circus, a Ferris wheel, and a white carousel horse. It's a friend for a lifetime. It's the smell of hot chocolate and the touch of soft velvet. It's the memory of someone I'll hold in my heart until I take my last dying breath. It's a small café theatre and the smell of espresso. It's cowboys and Indians and Elvis. It's balsam fir and black spruce in a forest.

It's summer and I'm in a comfortable chair. The radiator in front of the open window is turned off until winter, and I have an unobstructed view of the sky. I can see it from every angle. A sky so immense in its vastness that it could swallow a continent without even thinking. There are no curtains and the ledge is empty. I look at the top of the sky—if there's a top—rather than down to whatever happens to be at the bottom. It's a window with a clear view of the sky. I could be anywhere.

It's just before the creation of day, and it's the colour of almost blue. It's a fine summer morning—earth is just waking. It's noon and a church is ringing the angelus bell. It's dusk and there's a lavender light all over the world and everyone speaks in a whisper. It's all the little streets we walked as a child and those little streets were the universe. It's the dead of dark night and the moon is hanging from an invisible string. Stars are scattered like pinpoints on velvet, none overlapping—each with its own special place in the universe. There's a key to locating everything up in the sky, but you have to know where to look. You have to understand how sky operates.

I'm trying to piece every shred of my life back together again—if there ever was a before.

It's St. Patrick's Day and the Empire State Building is in three shades of emerald. It's Easter and it's purple and gold. It's Christmas—red, silver, and green. It's a Newfoundland hamlet and a roaring wild ocean. The waves are choppy and the sea has gone wild. It's the cry of a seagull and the smell of salt water. It's misty and the fog is as thick as pea soup. It's a thousand glass windows—thousands of landscapes. It's everyone I've ever met in my life. It's snow and rain and clouds and failure. It's the sweet touch of success when it happens. It's street lights and shop lights and lights in a small vest-pocket park. Lights of the traffic. It's everything that ever entered my life—everything that quickly passed through or stayed for a lifetime. It's torture and joy. It's today and tomorrow and it's all on a tiny dot floating in space—a dot that's so small that if we happened to be on the moon, instead of the earth, looking down, we could block out that dot with our thumb. Just imagine.

It's midnight and dew covers everything. It's a forest of silver birch and somebody praying. It's everything that we are and ever will be. It's *How are ye gettin' on, my luv? You're as welcome as the angels in heaven.*

It's a cup of hot tea and something homemade at the end of the day. And it's everything in between.

Acknowledgements

I would like to first and foremost thank Brian Henderson, director of Wilfrid Laurier University Press, for his continued and unwavering support, his wisdom, kindness, and encouragement—I am privileged to be a part of the Wilfrid Laurier University Press family. Thank you to my copy editor, Sara Murphy, for her patient attention to every word I'd been trying to say, and who often knew what I was trying to say before I did. Thank you to the entire amazing staff of Wilfrid Laurier University Press—especially Rob Kohlmeier, Leslie Macredie, Lisa Quinn, and Clare Hitchens, who never tired of my endless questions—for their help with every aspect of *Street Angel*. I am in debt to James Gossage and Michael Townsend Smith—treasured friends since the 1960s—for their friendship and patient input as they read draft after draft after draft of *Street Angel* and offered insight and unwavering encouragement. I will always be grateful to Anne Burke, a writer and the editor of *Prairie Journal* in Calgary. She has been a source of inspiration, encouragement, and friendship for almost three decades. Thank you to The Writers Room in New York for the quiet space where much of this book was written. Thank you to the author Nancy Milford for her inspiration and encouragement. Thank you to cherished friends and soulmates from a small café theatre in New York called the Caffe Cino. The café is gone now, as are many of the people, but its soul and energy are eternal and with me always. Thank you to a rugged, majestic, fearless, and exquisitely beautiful island called Newfoundland—my home. I carry that strength with me wherever I go. And thank you most especially to my daughter, Heather Rose, who was born in Newfoundland on a quiet, snow-covered morning, and who loves the ocean and snow and the infinite wonders of nature as much as I do. I am beyond blessed. Beyond, beyond!

A brief excerpt from Chapter 1 was published in the form of an essay, under a different title, in *Prairie Journal* in 2013, and was later nominated for the Pushcart Prize.

Glossary of Newfoundland Terms

Beothuk: the aboriginal people of the island of Newfoundland

best kind: great; awesome

brin bags: sacks made of burlap

b'y: means boy but is pronounced *by* (as in *down by the river*)

by and by: later

dropping *h*'s: a linguistic tendency, prevalent in parts of Newfoundland; not sounding *h* at the beginning of words where it ought to be sounded (*how* is pronounced *'ow*, and *house* is pronounced *'ouse*, with the inflection of *douse*, for instance)

fairy buns: bread that lone travellers carry to keep evil fairies away

fish flake: a high platform built on poles and used for drying codfish

gunshot away: a short distance

in a hobble: in a state of extreme worry

mauzy: foggy, damp, misty, or muggy (weather)

outport: in Newfoundland, any small, isolated fishing village

partridgeberry: the Newfoundland name for a plant most commonly known in English as a lingonberry or cowberry, which bears edible red fruit that is very popular for making jams and pies

scrunchions: small fried pieces of pork fat

to beat the band: forcefully, or in large quantities

woodhorse: a device for holding logs while they are being sawed into firewood-size pieces

Books in the Life Writing Series

Published by Wilfrid Laurier University Press

Haven't Any News: Ruby's Letters from the Fifties edited by Edna Staebler with an Afterword by Marlene Kadar • 1995 / x + 165 pp. / ISBN 0-88920-248-6

"I Want to Join Your Club": Letters from Rural Children, 1900–1920 edited by Norah L. Lewis with a Preface by Neil Sutherland • 1996 / xii + 250 pp. (30 b&w photos) / ISBN 0-88920-260-5

And Peace Never Came by Elisabeth M. Raab with Historical Notes by Marlene Kadar • 1996 / x + 196 pp. (12 b&w photos, map) / ISBN 0-88920-281-8

Dear Editor and Friends: Letters from Rural Women of the North-West, 1900–1920 edited by Norah L. Lewis • 1998 / xvi + 166 pp. (20 b&w photos) / ISBN 0-88920-287-7

The Surprise of My Life: An Autobiography by Claire Drainie Taylor with a Foreword by Marlene Kadar • 1998 / xii + 268 pp. (8 colour photos and 92 b&w photos) / ISBN 0-88920-302-4

Memoirs from Away: A New Found Land Girlhood by Helen M. Buss / Margaret Clarke • 1998 / xvi + 153 pp. / ISBN 0-88920-350-4

The Life and Letters of Annie Leake Tuttle: Working for the Best by Marilyn Färdig Whiteley • 1999 / xviii + 150 pp. / ISBN 0-88920-330-x

Marian Engel's Notebooks: "Ah, mon cahier, écoute" edited by Christl Verduyn • 1999 / viii + 576 pp. / ISBN 0-88920-333-4 cloth / ISBN 0-88920-349-0 paper

Be Good Sweet Maid: The Trials of Dorothy Joudrie by Audrey Andrews • 1999 / vi + 276 pp. / ISBN 0-88920-334-2

Working in Women's Archives: Researching Women's Private Literature and Archival Documents edited by Helen M. Buss and Marlene Kadar • 2001 / vi + 120 pp. / ISBN 0-88920-341-5

Repossessing the World: Reading Memoirs by Contemporary Women by Helen M. Buss • 2002 / xxvi + 206 pp. / ISBN 0-88920-408-x cloth / ISBN 0-88920-410-1 paper

Chasing the Comet: A Scottish-Canadian Life by Patricia Koretchuk • 2002 / xx + 244 pp. / ISBN 0-88920-407-1

The Queen of Peace Room by Magie Dominic • 2002 / xii + 115 pp. / ISBN 0-88920-417-9

China Diary: The Life of Mary Austin Endicott by Shirley Jane Endicott • 2002 / xvi + 251 pp. / ISBN 0-88920-412-8

The Curtain: Witness and Memory in Wartime Holland by Henry G. Schogt • 2003 / xii + 132 pp. / ISBN 0-88920-396-2

Teaching Places by Audrey J. Whitson • 2003 / xiii + 178 pp. / ISBN 0-88920-425-x

Through the Hitler Line by Laurence F. Wilmot, M.C. • 2003 / xvi + 152 pp. / ISBN 0-88920-448-9

Where I Come From by Vijay Agnew • 2003 / xiv + 298 pp. / ISBN 0-88920-414-4

The Water Lily Pond by Han Z. Li • 2004 / x + 254 pp. / ISBN 0-88920-431-4

The Life Writings of Mary Baker McQuesten: Victorian Matriarch edited by Mary J. Anderson • 2004 / xxii + 338 pp. / ISBN 0-88920-437-3

Seven Eggs Today: The Diaries of Mary Armstrong, 1859 and 1869 edited by Jackson W. Armstrong • 2004 / xvi + 228 pp. / ISBN 0-88920-440-3

Love and War in London: A Woman's Diary 1939–1942 by Olivia Cockett; edited by Robert W. Malcolmson • 2005 / xvi + 208 pp. / ISBN 0-88920-458-6

Incorrigible by Velma Demerson • 2004 / vi + 178 pp. / ISBN 0-88920-444-6

Auto/biography in Canada: Critical Directions edited by Julie Rak • 2005 / viii + 264 pp. / ISBN 0-88920-478-0

Tracing the Autobiographical edited by Marlene Kadar, Linda Warley, Jeanne Perreault, and Susanna Egan • 2005 / viii + 280 pp. / ISBN 0-88920-476-4

Must Write: Edna Staebler's Diaries edited by Christl Verduyn • 2005 / viii + 304 pp. / ISBN 0-88920-481-0

Pursuing Giraffe: A 1950s Adventure by Anne Innis Dagg • 2006 / xvi + 284 pp. (photos, 2 maps) / 978-0-88920-463-8

Food That Really Schmecks by Edna Staebler • 2007 / xxiv + 334 pp. / ISBN 978-0-88920-521-5

163256: A Memoir of Resistance by Michael Englishman • 2007 / xvi + 112 pp. (14 b&w photos) / ISBN 978-1-55458-009-5

The Wartime Letters of Leslie and Cecil Frost, 1915–1919 edited by R.B. Fleming • 2007 / xxxvi + 384 pp. (49 b&w photos, 5 maps) / ISBN 978-1-55458-000-2

Johanna Krause Twice Persecuted: Surviving in Nazi Germany and Communist East Germany by Carolyn Gammon and Christiane Hemker • 2007 / x + 170 pp. (58 b&w photos, 2 maps) / ISBN 978-1-55458-006-4

Watermelon Syrup: A Novel by Annie Jacobsen with Jane Finlay-Young and Di Brandt • 2007 / x + 268 pp. / ISBN 978-1-55458-005-7

Broad Is the Way: Stories from Mayerthorpe by Margaret Norquay • 2008 / x + 106 pp. (6 b&w photos) / ISBN 978-1-55458-020-0

Becoming My Mother's Daughter: A Story of Survival and Renewal by Erika Gottlieb • 2008 / x + 178 pp. (36 b&w illus., 17 colour) / ISBN 978-1-55458-030-9

Leaving Fundamentalism: Personal Stories edited by G. Elijah Dann • 2008 / xii + 234 pp. / ISBN 978-1-55458-026-2

Bearing Witness: Living with Ovarian Cancer edited by Kathryn Carter and Lauri Elit • 2009 / viii + 94 pp. / ISBN 978-1-55458-055-2

Dead Woman Pickney: A Memoir of Childhood in Jamaica by Yvonne Shorter Brown • 2010 / viii + 202 pp. / ISBN 978-1-55458-189-4

I Have a Story to Tell You by Seemah C. Berson • 2010 / xx + 288 pp. (24 b&w photos) / ISBN 978-1-55458-219-8

We All Giggled: A Bourgeois Family Memoir by Thomas O. Hueglin • 2010 / xiv + 232 pp. (20 b&w photos) / ISBN 978-1-55458-262-4

Just a Larger Family: Letters of Marie Williamson from the Canadian Home Front, 1940–1944 edited by Mary F. Williamson and Tom Sharp • 2011 / xxiv + 378 pp. (16 b&w photos) / ISBN 978-1-55458-323-2

Burdens of Proof: Faith, Doubt, and Identity in Autobiography by Susanna Egan • 2011 / x + 200 pp. / ISBN 978-1-55458-333-1

Accident of Fate: A Personal Account 1938–1945 by Imre Rochlitz with Joseph Rochlitz • 2011 / xiv + 226 pp. (50 b&w photos, 5 maps) / ISBN 978-1-55458-267-9

The Green Sofa by Natascha Würzbach, translated by Raleigh Whitinger • 2012 / xiv + 240 pp. (5 b&w photos) / ISBN 978-1-55458-334-8

Unheard Of: Memoirs of a Canadian Composer by John Beckwith • 2012 / x + 393 pp. (74 illus., 8 musical examples) / ISBN 978-1-55458-358-4

Borrowed Tongues: Life Writing, Migration, and Translation by Eva C. Karpinski • 2012 / viii + 274 pp. / ISBN 978-1-55458-357-7

Basements and Attics, Closets and Cyberspace: Explorations in Canadian Women's Archives edited by Linda M. Morra and Jessica Schagerl • 2012 / x + 338 pp. / ISBN 978-1-55458-632-5

The Memory of Water by Allen Smutylo • 2013 / x + 262 pp. (65 colour illus.) / ISBN 978-1-55458-842-8

The Unwritten Diary of Israel Unger, Revised Edition by Carolyn Gammon and Israel Unger •2013 / ix + 230 pp. (b&w illus.) / ISBN 978-1-77112-011-1

Boom! Manufacturing Memoir for the Popular Public by Julie Rak • 2013 / viii + 249 pp. (b&w illus.) / ISBN 978-1-55458-939-5

Motherlode: A Mosaic of Dutch Wartime Experience by Carolyne Van Der Meer • 2014 / xiv + 132 pp. (b&w illus.) / ISBN 978-1-77112-005-0

Not the Whole Story: Challenging the Single Mother Narrative edited by Lea Caragata and Judit Alcalde • 2014 / x + 222 pp. / ISBN 978-1-55458-624-0

Street Angel by Magie Dominic • 2014 / viii + 154 pp. / ISBN 978-1-77112-026-5